RYEDALE RE...

by

Peter Brears

Ryedale Folk Museum
&
Hutton Press Ltd.
1998

Published by
the Ryedale Folk Museum,
Hutton-le-Hole, North Yorkshire

and the Hutton Press Ltd.,
130 Canada Drive, Cherry Burton,
Beverley HU17 7SB

Printed and bound by Fretwells Limited,
Hull

ISBN 1 872167 96 9

Front cover: Making oatcakes, and cooking a complete dinner in an iron cauldron, in John Huntley's early eighteenth century house from Stang End, Danby. It now stands in the Ryedale Folk Museum at Hutton-le-Hole.
                    Photo courtesy Richard Clive

Back cover: A selection of tea-time foods from Victorian Ryedale, seen in the Harome Cottage, at the Ryedale Folk Museum.
                    Photo courtesy Richard Clive

Frontispiece: Today we take our kitchen units, gas and electic cookers, water on tap, good lighting and many other modern conveniences for granted, but here William Hayes' photograph shows how Mrs Elizabeth Harland, like most local housewives, managed to produce all her family's food in conditions which were far from ideal. This photograph was taken at The Mount, Hutton-le-Hole about 1910.

CONTENTS

Introduction

Ryedale has always been one of Yorkshire's most fertile regions, being centred on the broad Vale of Pickering, with the North York Moors to the north, the Wolds to the south, and the Howardian Hills to the west. Back in the early sixteenth century, John Leland described its 'Hille and Dale meate plentifull of Corn and Grasse, but litle Wood in sight', while William Marshall's pioneering *Rural Economy of Yorkshire* of 1788 celebrated its pure water, its fine cattle, pigs, sheep and rabbits, its barley, oats and root crops, its butter and its cheese.[1] It was also a great fruit-growing area, while on the Moors in particular bees provided plentiful supplies of honey.

Most of the food grown here was sent away by cart, by barges along the Derwent navigation, and later by the railways, either to provision ships sailing out of ports such as Whitby, or to feed the workers in the great manufacturing centres of the West Riding. Substantial quantities still remained in Ryedale, however, where they maintained everyone from the farm labourers, the farmers, squires and major landowners, to the craftsmen and merchants, who all played their part in keeping Ryedale fertile, productive and prosperous.

In every household, the housewife, cook or housekeeper developed a whole range of distinctive recipes which made the most of the local resources of food and fuel. Those which she had learned in childhood, and made virtually every week, she knew by heart, but those made only from time to time, or which she had sampled in the homes of her friends and relations, were often noted down in her recipe book. Quite often these recipes contained only a brief list of the ingredients, since she already knew the methods, and therefore had no need to write them down in detail. Similarly, she knew by experience how to adjust her recipes according to the size of her eggs etc, and how to control her oven, poking the fire or moving the damper as necessary, and then confirming whether the oven was either 'quick','moderate' or 'slow' merely by opening the door and inserting her hand to judge the level of the heat.

During the years between the wars, this traditional form of cookery began to change. Increased mechanisation on the farms, especially the move from horses to tractors, meant that the numbers of living-in farm servants dropped dramatically. Modern gas, electric and oil cookers began to replace the old wood, turf or coal-heated ranges, while new stainless steel, plastic and electric-powered equipment replaced the old cast iron, wood and hand-operated utensils. Home cooking tended to go into a decline too, as tinned, frozen, dried, and pre-cooked foods began to appear first in grocer's shops, and later in the supermarkets.

As early as the 1930s Mr R.Wilfrid Crosland, a lecturer who worked for the W.E.A., had realised that evidence of the old ways of life was already beginning to disappear, and by 1935 had collected sufficient 'Ryedale Items of Interest, Historical Relics'"Bygones", Photographs and Printed Notices and Old Records, etc.,etc.' to form a private Ryedale Museum at his house 'Elphield', next to the Crown Inn in Hutton le Hole. Later, from 1961, Mr Bert Frank, a native of Hutton le Hole whose family had lived there from at least the sixteenth century, built up another fine collection of Ryedale material at nearby Lastingham. Following Mr Crosland's death in 1963, and that of his surviving sister in 1964, 'Elphield' and its collection were bequeathed to Mr Frank, who moved into the property with his collection, and immediately opened the Ryedale Folk Museum to the public. At that time only three rooms were on show, but the museum soon became a charitable trust, the Crosland Foundation, and began to expand rapidly. Over the next fifteen years Mr Frank led a team of scores of skilled and enthusiastic volunteers who not only collected thousands of individual folklife specimens from the Ryedale area, but also moved complete buildings to the museum, these including cruck cottages, a manor house, farm buildings, a sixteenth century glass kiln etc. Since then the museum has continued to flourish, winning the 1995 Museum of the Year Award in competition with museums from all parts of Britain.

Many of the items collected by the museum are connected with Ryedale food and cookery. These range from locally-made fireplaces and ovens, to furniture, cooking pots and all manner of utensils. Although most of these are on display in the various period interiors, and Mrs Dorothy Ellison has completed a full card index of everything in the museum, there is still a need to present a full catalogue of them, identifying them and presenting all their related information both to visitors, and to everyone else who is interested in this subject. The individual number of each item is given in brackets in the following chapters, so that further details can be looked up in the Catalogue section. The museum also has a number of handwritten recipe books which cannot be put on permanent display, since they would fade in the light. For these reasons, this book has been written to provide a detailed account of the traditional cookery of Ryedale, particularly during the nineteenth and early twentieth centuries. A selection of the original recipes has been re-written in modern form, with both Imperial and metric measurements and oven temperatures etc., and with their sizes reduced to suit the needs of today's households (when few of us cook by the gallon or peck!), but still retaining the original methods and the proportions of ingredients, so that they can all be reproduced as authentically as possible. They range from the simplest and most economical of dishes, through to the most luxurious, but all represent part of this region's rich culinary tradition.

I hope that this book will encourage a greater interest in Ryedale and its recipes, and that anyone with information or recipes etc. from this area will consider passing them on to the Ryedale Folk Museum at Hutton le Hole.

Peter Brears
Leeds, 1998

Acknowledgements

This publication has received grant-aid from the Yorkshire & Humberside Museums Council and the Sophie Coe Prize, 1997.

I would like to thank Mr Martin Watts, Curator of the Ryedale Folk Museum, and his staff, for all their help, and coffees, when working at the museum, and to Mrs Dorothy Ellison, Assistant Curator, who has spent many years documenting the collection to the highest standards. I am also grateful to Mr Richard Clive for undertaking the colour photography for this book, and to Beamish Museum for the photograph of Spout House.

I am especially grateful to Mrs E. Frank and Mr R. Frank, wife and son of the late Mr Bert Frank, for permission to publish both his description of wood, peat and turf in Ryedale, and also their family recipes for gale beer etc. In addition, the memories of Mr Raymond Hayes and Mr David Wood have proved invaluable.

Many thanks are also due to Mr & Mrs G. Fairhurst of the Barn Hotel, Hutton le Hole, not only for providing such comfortable accommodation and splendid meals, but also for their permission to copy and publish a number of the recipes written by Miss H.Crosland who lived at 'Elphield', the present Ryedale Folk Museum, from the 1930s to the 1960s.

The fireplace at Stang End, now rebuilt at the Ryedale Folk Museum, shows all the typical local features, including the smoke hood (1), the witch post (2), the heck (3), the spice box and salt box (4 & 5), the rannlebauk (6), reckon (7), and early form of yetling (8), and the fire window which illuminated the hearth.

Spout House, the old Sun Inn in Bilsdale, still has its stone bread oven, the square hatch to the left of the fireplace. It is remembered that it was heated up in the evening with coals and embers from the fire, these being raked out last thing at night, and the bread put in, so that it would emerge beautifully baked next morning. Once, for a bet, the local policeman managed to fit himself inside this oven.

Traditional Cookery

In many parts of Ryedale, particularly along the southern edge of the Moors, most of the cooking was carried out over turf (peat) or wood fires up to the 1940s. Although collecting these fuels was both time-consuming and laborious, they cost virtually nothing at a time when coal was quite expensive, and gas was a thing of the future, and then only within the towns. For centuries local housewives had prepared all their families' food over smouldering turves heaped on the flat stone hearths of their farm or cottage kitchens. Where wood was available, the fires may have been raised on firedogs to stop the logs rolling forward and to provide a good under-draught, but essentially all cooking had to be done over a small, floor-level bonfire. Hearths of this type usually had a small window to one side to light the cooking area, a stone salt-box (1) being built into the fireplace wall between the window and the fire itself.[1] Here salt would keep perfectly dry and ready for use, an oak door swinging on either dowels or leather strap hinges (since salt would corrode iron or brass) keeping out all steam, dirt or condensation. Some houses had a small spice cupboard inserted just above the saltbox, as at John Huntley's improved house of 1704 at Stang End (2).

If there was sufficient radiant heat, food could be placed on one of the half-round roasters made by the Wedgwood family at their Yearsley pottery between Hovingham and Easingwold. Two of these dated 1712 and 1726 are in the York museums.[2] It was easier, however, to cook the food in a cast-iron vessel hung from an adjustable pot-hook or *reckon* suspended from a *rannlebauk,* a wooden bar fixed across the chimney.[3] These had to be treated with some respect, being kept brightly polished as a sure sign of good housekeeping, and never being allowed to swing to and fro for;[4]

'When any maydes take the potte of the fyer in greate haste she setts yt downe, and, without feare of burninge clappes her hands on the pot-hookes to stay them from shakeing: and this she does tender hearty believinge that our Lady weepeth or greeteth, as thee term yt, all the while the pottehookes waggle, which were lamentable case.'

For boiling joints of fresh or salt beef, mutton, or the traditionally-cured fat bacon, a large cast iron pot or cauldron was half-filled with water and hung over the fire. If the meat was salted, it was put in immediately, but if it was fresh, it was put in when the water had boiled, remaining there for about 15 minutes for every pound it weighed, all scum being carefully removed to stop it spoiling the meat. Vegetables, perhaps contained in a string bag so that they could easily be lifted out and drained, were added at a later stage, so that they would be ready at precisely the same time as the meat. A pudding could also be boiled in the pot at the same time, the following example of 1806, a favourite accompaniment to ham or pork, coming from the recipe book of Dr Hunter of York.[5]

Pease Pudding
350g (12 oz)   yellow split peas
25g (1 oz)   butter
15ml (1 tbs)   cream
2 eggs, beaten
pepper and salt
1. tie the peas loosely in a muslin cloth, soak for at least an hour, then simmer them until they become tender
2. rub them through a sieve, stir the remaining ingredients
3. take a square of cotton, flannel or doubled muslin , scald it, squeeze it dry, sprinkle the

upper side with flour, shake off the surplus, place it across a two-pint basin, fill with the mixture, close the cloth over the pudding, and tie it securely
4. Lift the pudding from the basin, plunge it into a deep pan of boiling water, and boil for 30 minutes before draining it, and turning it out into a warm dish

Fairly plain fruit puddings such as Jane Trenham's Fig Pudding could also be boiled with the meat;

Fig Pudding
225g (8 oz) dried figs, chopped
225g (8 oz) fresh breadcrumbs
100g (4 oz) suet
100g (4 oz) brown sugar
50g (2 oz) plain flour
2 eggs, beaten
1.25ml ($^1/_4$ tsp) grated nutmeg
110ml (4 fl. oz.) milk
1. mix together all the dry ingredients with just enough milk to form a stiff paste
2. tie in a cloth (see 3 in the last recipe) and boil for 2 hours

When everything in the pot had cooked to perfection, the broth was ladled out to form the first course, this being followed by the fruited pudding, perhaps accompanied with brandy sauce. Next came the hot meat and savoury or peas pudding, these perhaps being followed by oven-baked bilberry and apple tarts to complete an extremely good dinner.

Other rich and flavoursome dishes boiled in the iron pot included sheep's head broth, or the following mutton broth entered in the Middleton Lodge recipe book in the 1860s. It starts off by taking meat and vegetables, simmering them long and slow to make a fine stock, then adding fresh meat, vegetables and dumplings which were then simmered to tenderness. It is an ideal meal for a country household, the final ingredients being added whenever people come in from the cold winter weather, and being ready just when they have thawed out, and will appreciate something really good and warming.

Mutton Broth
4 leeks   *for the dumplings;*
4 heads of celery   *225g (8 oz) plain flour*
4 turnips   *225g (8 oz) suet*
50g (2 oz) rice   *3 eggs, beaten*
450g (16 oz) neck of mutton,
about 3 small lamb chops per person
1. coarsely chop half the vegetables, place them in a large pan with the neck of mutton and half the rice, cover with water, and simmer gently for 6-8 hours, adding more water as needed
2. when the stock is ready, trim the bones and fat from the chops, beat the lean lightly, then add to the stock, along with the remaining rice and the vegetables, sliced
3. mix the flour and suet, stir in the eggs to form a stiff dough, form into dumplings and drop these into the stock when it has returned to a brisk simmer
4. simmer for a further 30 minutes until the meat, dumplings etc are cooked, then serve

Raymond Hayes can remember a similar meal about the time of the First World War. He and six friends were walking on the Moors, when they found that one of them had brought no lunch. At first they thought that he would have to go without, since there were neither shops nor inns nearby. However, on asking at an isolated farmhouse, they were invited in by the farmer's wife, who had an iron pot simmering over the peat fire, which contained two chickens, vegetables and dumplings, the latter being pulled out of the broth on their individual strings. There was enough to feed them all. At the end of the meal they were asked if they liked rice pudding. On hearing that they did, she scooped up the rice from the bottom of the pot, and served it out for them.

As these descriptions show, very good food can be produced using the simplest of utensils. The same is true with baking. There was once a soft oatcake, or *havercake* tradition here, for Ryedale was the major oat-producing region of Yorkshire, and the implements used for making soft oatcakes or havercakes are found locally. Following the usual method found in the Dales and West Yorkshire, the fine oatmeal would be mixed with water or buttermilk and allowed to ferment overnight using a sourdough method, or by adding yeast, In the morning, a ladle-full (66) would be poured on to a bed of dry oatmeal scattered across the diamond-grooved surface of a large, flat wooden *riddleboard* (114). This prevented the batter from sticking to the wood as it was reeled around with a circular motion to form a thin, round liquid cake. which could then be slid directly onto a hot *turfstone* or *backston,* a slab of stone heated over the fire. This implement is described in the lines of the local ballad of 'The Maid of the Golden Shoon', handed down from before1700, collected from Mistress Bessy Ellis (c.1763-1840) by the Vicar or Curate of Lastingham or Cropton around 1815, and shortly after included in a Mell Act written by Robert Cooper, licensee of the Crown Inn, Hutton le Hole;

'But serve ye your best of food and of rest...
Let not your turfstones cool;
From your rafter string let your havver cake hing...'

while William Marshall called it 'a slate, hung on an iron frame over the fire, to bake cakes on'.[6] Later examples were made of iron (117-122). Alternatively, the batter could be slid onto a piece of flannel resting on a square, bat-like *spittle* (111-113) and then, with great skill, thrown onto the backston to give a much thinner cake. Whichever method was used, the oatcake was then freed from the backston, turned over to briefly cook the other side, and then hung up to dry out ready for being eaten fresh, or dried out to crispness for eating later.

It comes as no surprise that rye was Ryedale's main bread crop for many centuries up to the mid eighteenth century. Writing in 1800, John Tuke described how 'a very black, heavy, sour bread was made of rye [Black rye up to around 1750, when White or Danzig rye was introduced], and is not entirely out of date among the lower orders of the country'. This was the identical sourdough ryebread which we now think of as being an essentially German, Scandinavian or Jewish product. To make it, 'a large tub, called a kimlin, is provided; this being only scraped, and not washed out, after each time of using, the paste which remains on the sides becomes sour; in this vessel one half of the meal intended to be used, is mixed with water in the evening; this is covered up with some dry meal, and lies in sponge till morning; in that time, the tub has communicated its acidity to the whole mass, which causes a fermentation similar to that produced by yeast; it is worked up stiff with the remainder of the meal; this is often done with the feet, the dough being covered with a coarse cloth; after it has thus been well worked, it is made into large loaves, and set in the oven, where it remains about ten or twelve hours. As this kind of bread will keep a considerable time, it is made in large quantities at once, three bushels at a baking is frequent, which quantity is made into seven or eight large loaves; many farmers do not make this bread more than four, or six times in the year.'[7]

Loaves of this type, weighing up to 18 lb each continued to be baked in sheet-iron loaf tins up to the late nineteenth century.[8] In most households, however, it had been replaced by maslin bread made from a mixed crop of wheat and rye, threshed, winnowed and ground together to make meal. As Tuke recorded, 'Of maslin, the common household or brown bread is made in families of every rank in the country, and more wholesome or nutritious bread cannot be used; no perceptible flavour or difference arises from the mixture of the rye, and the only effect it has is to render the bread somewhat longer from growing stale'.[9]

The following modern recipe produces a loaf very similar to the traditional Yorkshire maslin bread.

Maslin Bread

450g (16oz) rye meal
675g (1 lb 8 oz) strong wheat flour, 85 or 100% wholemeal
575ml (1 pt) water at 40°C, 100°F
10g (1/2 oz) salt
25g (1 oz) yeast
1. mix half the meal and flour with half the water, and stand in a warm place for 12 to 16 hours
2. mix the remaining meal, flour and the salt in a bowl, and place in a very low oven until they have become slightly warm
3. put the yeast into a cup, pour on sufficient warm water to just cover it, leave it for about five minutes, then mix to form a cream
4. remove the dry flour etc from the oven, make a well in the centre, pour in the yeast, and some of the remaining warm water, stir it with a spoon, then add the rest of the water, and knead with the hands for a few minutes
5. add the sourdough from 1, and knead them together to form an elastic dough which comes away from the sides of the bowl, adding more flour if neccesary
6. cover the bread with a warm dish, or a piece of polythene and leave in a warm place to rise for about 1½-2 hours
7. punch it down and knead it on a floured board for 3-4 minutes, then form it into two round cobs, cover them with a light cloth, and leave them in a warm place to prove for a further 1½ hours
8. pre-heat the oven to 220°C, 425°F, gas mark 7, cook the bread for 20 minutes, then reduce it to 205°C, 400°C, gas mark 5, for a further 40-50 minutes until it is baked. The crust will probably crack, this being a characteristic of this kind of bread

Up to about 1780, Ryedale had to bring in much of its supplies of wheat from Cleveland, wagon loads coming over the Moors to the weekly market at Kirkby Moorside.[10] By 1800 this situation was reversed, as wheat grown in Ryedale not only met local demands, but was sent both to Whitby market, and to Malton, from where it was sent down the Derwent and up the Aire to Leeds, Wakefield, and the other West Riding towns. Similar changes affected the Wolds about this time. Around 1800 Capt. Anderson of Kilham had written that;[11]

'On Yorkshire Wolds we mostly barley eat,
For there they grow but very little wheat;

We live on barley bread and barley pies,
And oats and peas the want of wheat supplies'

Heavy, dry and greyish, barley bread became increasingly unpopular as the newly-improved Wolds developed into the country's finest wheat-producing area, but even at the beginning of the twentieth century, there were still a number of farm labourers who could remember dire meals of;

'Barley bread, barley pies,
Mouldy bacon and cheese with eyes!'

In the largest houses wheat flour had been used for virtually all kinds of bakery for centuries, the wholemeal being used for household bread, and the finer white flours for white bread, cakes and pastries. A *temce,* or coarse sieve, separated the coarser meal from the bran, a *tiffany,* or fine gauze sieve, then separating out the finer white flour.[12]

The wholemeal loaves in the following recipe were probably intended for the servants.[13]

Castle Howard Brown Bread, 1755

900g (2 lb) strong wholewheat flour
25g (1 oz) yeast
575ml (1 pt) milk at 40°C, 100°F
575ml (1 pt) water at 40°C, 100°F
1. put 675g (1 lb 8oz) of the flour into a bowl and place in a very low oven until warm
2. put the yeast into a cup, pour on just sufficient water to cover it, leave for 5 minutes, then mix to form a smooth cream
3. remove the flour from the oven, make a well in the centre, pour in the yeast, milk and water, stir to form a smooth paste, cover with a warm dish or piece of polythene, and leave to rise for 15 minutes
4. Knead in sufficient additional flour, about ¹/₂lb, to form a dough, knead it on a floured board for a few minutes until it becomes elastic, then return to the bowl, cover it once more, and leave it in a warm place for 1¹/₂ hours
5. proceed as from 7 in the maslin bread recipe on the previous page.

Some local houses, such as Spout House in Bilsdale, had built-in bread ovens, their domed masonry interiors being heated by faggots of burning brushwood, which were raked out just before the bread was put in. In many cottages and farmhouses, it is most likely that bread was baked either amid the glowing embers arranged on the hearthstone with a *cowl-rake* (175-177), or on a *backston* which, in the 1890s, Richard Blakeborough described as 'A sheet of iron, sometimes a stone, having an iron hoop to hang it over the fire by, and used to bake cakes upon'.[14] This could produce good oatcakes, and breadcakes and scones too, if they were relatively thin and were turned over half-way through baking. Its main problem was that, unlike an oven, it could not provide any top-heat. To remedy this, a whole tradition of cooking was developed which used iron pots which could be hung over the fire from a reckon.

For fairly flat cakes etc. a deep frying pan was used (122). Once it had been heated up, the cakes were placed inside, and a domed cast-iron lid put on, its raised rim holding a heap of burning embers on top, so that the cakes were baked evenly from both above and from below. A visitor to the Chequers Inn, Slapestones, described such a pan with its 'iron cover over the top, on which glowing pieces of turf are laid whilst underneath is the turf fire. The cakes by this method are beautifully browned on both sides'.[15] When Mrs Smith, a cook at one of the Moors farms at the end of the nineteenth century, wanted to use her frying pan to bake 'bread, meat, meat pies etc., she had a wide middle rim, like a small cart hoop, which used to fit between the two shallow pans, and so made room for anything bulky (123). And all these things cooked this way were most delicious and had a flavour all of their own'.

Alternatively, a deep cylindrical cast-iron pot with three short legs and a bow handle was used for this purpose. This was known as a *yetling*. This word, used from the fourteenth century throughout the Scottish Lowlands, the Borders and North East England, originally described a cooking pot of the traditional cauldron shape, but here became firmly associated with the cylindrical shape known elsewhere as a camp kettle. When Michael Heavisides saw his dinner being cooked at Stingamires in Bilsdale, he noted that 'The large camp-kettle is on the fire...This kettle has an iron cover, and hot embers of turf are placed on it, thus it receives the heat from the top and the bottom. The dinners cooked are A1'.[16]

Mrs Smith's daughter, Miss Green of Thornton Dale, continued to use her mother's recipes for girdle and yetling bakery, these including;

Flap Cakes (Sad Cakes)
225g (8 oz) plain flour
75g (3 oz) butter or lard
5ml (1 tsp) baking powder
45-60ml (3-4tbs) milk
1. sift the baking powder into the flour, rub in the butter or lard, and mix in sufficient milk to form a firm dough
2. roll out the dough into a large round, and either cook on a girdle until brown on one side, then turn over and cook on the other, or bake at 200°C, 400°F, gas mark 6 for 10 minutes
3. serve hot, splitting it open, spreading the inside with butter, and perhaps Golden Syrup too

Turf or Girdle Cakes
Make as Flap Cakes, but add 50g (2 oz) currants and 25g (1½ tbs) sugar if you wish. These were a favourite delicacy at many of the Moorland inns, especially the Wagon and Horses at Saltersgate.

Potato Cakes
225g (8 oz) mashed potatoes
75g (3 oz) plain flour
50g (2 oz) lard, beef dripping, or butter
5ml (1 tsp) baking powder
1. work all the ingredients together with a fork to form a smooth dough
2. roll out on a well-floured board to around a quarter to half an inch (1cm) in thickness, and bake first one side, and then the other, on an ungreased girdle until golden brown
3. serve either hot and buttered, or fry with bacon for breakfast

Ryedale was crossed by packhorse and wagon routes, and enjoyed good river transport facilities from Malton. Even so, the transport of heavy and bulky goods remained an extremely troublesome business up to the opening of the Whitby and Pickering Railway in 1835 and the York-Scarborough line in 1845. These gave ready access to the great Northumberland, Durham, West and South Yorkshire coalfields, whose supplies were far superior to those of the Moorland pits at Fryup Head, Danby, Blakey and Rudland. This new supply was especially appreciated in the Vale of Pickering, and on the Wolds, where there had always been a shortage of fuel.

Now that coal, coke, iron and similar raw materials were readily available, it was possible for an agricultural engineering industry to start in Ryedale, one of its products being cast-iron kitchen ranges. It is probable that some of the earliest ovens in Ryedale had been made around 1800 by the great Walker foundry in Rotherham, oven doors bearing this name and beautifully moulded trophies of harvest implements coming from Stingamires in Bilsdale and elsewhere in Ryedale (138). This foundry made the great iron bridge over the Wear at Sunderland in 1793-6, and could easily have introduced its products here via the flourishing coastal trade.

In the 1840s Isaac Hartas of the Wrelton Works, two miles north-west of Pickering, and Christopher Carter of the Ryedale Foundry at Kirkby Moorside, both began to manufacture ranges, their lead being followed by Dobson's and Fletcher's of Pickering and Henry Carter of the Cyclops Foundry, Kirkby Moorside. In most parts of northern England, kitchen ranges followed the classic Yorkshire pattern, with a central coal-burning grate which heated an oven to one side, a boiler either at the other side or in the fireback, and perhaps a raised shelf on which plates and dishes could be kept warm. In Ryedale many ranges were made to quite a different pattern, with two completely separate fires.

The main fire, which was used for keeping the house warm, drying clothes, boiling kettles, and cooking on backstons and yetlings, was now raised above the stone hearth on a large cast-iron turf-plate (129-134). At its centre, towards the back, a removable rectangular section cast with bars a quarter of an inch apart for turf, or half an inch apart for coal, fitted into the turf-plate, so that the fuel could now burn efficiently with a good draught from below, also leaving a space underneath to receive the ashes. These were extremely popular, hundreds being made in the local foundries from the 1840s through to the 1930s. To protect the fireback, and to provide a ready supply of hot water, L-shaped boilers were fitted along the back of the turfplate, one end extending towards the front, where a hinged lid was provided so that cold water could be poured in and hot water be ladled out as required.

For these ranges, masonry chimney stacks with rectangular openings, lintels, mantlepieces and fire-surrounds were needed, the old wood-framed smoke hoods either being replaced entirely, or having shallow masonry chimney stacks built within them. This certainly made the houses much more comfortable, keeping out both the winter winds and the rains which had driven billows of smoke and sooty splashes down the chimney. To give an even greater degree of protection, the upper part of the fireplace, just below the mantlepiece, was covered by an arch- or straight-bottomed stone slab. This ensured that the chimney did not smoke, and also kept the chimney crane and reckons clear of the rising fumes, making them much easier to keep clean and bright (140-174).

Where coal was the main fuel, raised grates with cast-iron firebars and brick firebacks were installed, just like those of the normal Yorkshire range (135-136), the open ash-pit now being covered by a 'Tidy Betty' which looked tidy, and prevented the wind, and potentially the children too, from disturbing the hot, fine cinders. The radiant heat from these coal-fired ranges was ideal for toasting, using either toasting forks (186-189), toasting dogs (191), toasters which hung from the firebars (190), or Dutch ovens (193-194). These had wire hooks hung within a shiny tinplate reflector, and could grill bacon, chops and kidneys, or cook eggs, melt cheese for rarebits, or make ham toast in their shallow drip-trays.

Ham Toast, Middleton Lodge
30ml (2 tbs) finely chopped boiled ham
30ml (2 tbs) chicken or pork gravy
30ml (2 tbs) cream
30ml (2 tbs) fresh chopped parsley
a few slices of fresh buttered toast
1. mix the ham, gravy, cream and breadcrumbs in a saucepan, and cook it slowly, stirring continuously, until it is fairly thick, and really hot
2. spread the mixture on the toast, sprinkle it with parsley, and place under a hot grill until the surface is lightly toasted

To support the Dutch ovens, kettles, saucepans and flat-irons in front of the firebars, a number of sad-iron heaters (179) or draw-plates (180-183) were used. Many of these items were made by Joseph Woodhead of Vaughan Street Works in Bradford. This company, founded in 1830, also produced reckon hooks (147-173), but these, along with chimney cranes (140-146), which swung from the side of the range, were usually made by the local ironfounders and blacksmiths. For cooking over the fire, iron pots and backstons could be stood on a set of briggs (178) propped between the top firebar and the fireback, grid-irons (200-203) for broiling thin cuts of meat or filleted fish either occupying the same position, or hanging from a reckon.

To complete the range, a baking oven was constructed to one side of the open fire (128,135-137). Beneath the oven itself were a pair of iron doors, the top one being for a firebox, where the coal or wood was burned, while the bottom one was for the ashpit, one or both doors having regulators to control the draught. From here, the heat rose around the back and sides of the oven, then passing through a damper controlled by a central knob just above the oven door. Two further knobs at each side were connected by long rods to an iron frame running around the top and sides of the oven. As it was pulled forwards, it scraped off all the soot which had accumulated on the oven, making sure that the oven received the full benefit of the heat, and reducing the risk of a chimney fire. Equipped with these ovens, the housewife could bake all the bread, cakes, pastries and pies required by her family. Even so, some of the old cooking methods were still retained, the flavour and economy of backston and yetling cookery ensuring that it continued well into the 1930s.

This drawing of the fireplace at Stingamires in Bilsdale around 1900 shows a wealth of detail. On the left, the black hole is the doorway of the salt box, while above the peat fire a yetling hangs from a reckon, the burning peats heaped on its lid ensuring that the food inside was evenly cooked. A boiler forms the back and side of the fire, water being baled from the lid in the top of the right-hand hob. The iron oven on the right is one of the earliest type found in Ryedale, probably being made by Walkers of Rotherham around 1800.

Farmhouse Food

'Hungery? Say ye? i' t'good awd tahmes?
Aye, bairn, Ah was hungery, allus, at yam when Ah was a lad:
Bud efter Ah went te farm-pleeacin, ye knaw, things wasn't se bad,
At ten year aed, i' t'good awd tahmes.

That was salvaation, i' t'good awd tahmes.
We reckoned nowt aboot wark, if we nobbut had plenty te eeat;
Suet pudden, an' broth, an' bacon, or butcher meeat;
'Twas grand, was that, i' t'good awd tahmes!'[1]

The writer of these verses was the Rev. Walter Turner, who grew up at Middleton near Pickering in the 1880s and '90s when his father was vicar there. He had seen first-hand how hard life was for the families of local 'daytal-chaps', the casual farm labourers who were paid by the day for their work. A typical day might start by leaving home before 4am, then walking four miles to the farm where work began at 5am, and it was rare that they were able to return home before 7 in the evening. For this they received their food while at the farm, and eight shillings (40p) a week on which to keep their growing families. Their wives and children also worked on the land, perhaps hoeing turnips, weeding, helping in the harvest field, or picking flints off the land, for which they were paid a shilling (5p) a ton, with a sad-cake for their dinners. Bread, a few vegetables, and bacon etc. provided by rearing a recklin, the weakest piglet in the litter begged from a farmer, made up their entire diet. Within the larger farmhouses, however, the farmers, their families and the farm servants who lived in with them received very substantial meals in order to enable them to complete their long days of hard physical labour.[2]

As the Vale of Pickering and the Wolds were brought into full agricultural production following their improvement in the late eighteenth century, their farms adopted a life-style which was to continue with little change over the next 150 years. On starting work in their early teens, most lads and lasses would attend the 'stattis' or hirings held in the market places of Helmsley, Kirkby Moorside, Pickering and Malton at Martinmas, November 23rd. Here, amid the fairground booths and lively public houses, they stood around, hoping to be selected by one of the farmers who had come here to find farm servants for the following year. If they were successful, they were given a sum of money, about half a crown (25p) in the 1920s, to seal the bargain, and then went off to enjoy a week's holiday at home before starting their new job. In the East Riding, the Sunday of this week was known as Rive-kite (ie tear-stomach) Sunday, when their mothers would prepare a really good dinner for them, with a roast goose if it could possibly be afforded, and hot ale possets. They would then pack up their belongings and travel to the farms where they were to complete a year's work before either staying on, or returning to the hirings once more. This decision might well depend on the quality of food they had received, whether it was a good living place or not. Around 1800 William Marshall stated that their diet was simple, 'Milk remains here a food of farm servants. In some places animal food (ie meat) three times a day is expected; here, once a day (except perhaps in haytime and harvest) is considered as sufficient. In malt liquor too, the farm servants of this country are equally moderate'.[3] Within a few years, however, meat was being served for three meals a day, the men needing this quality of food to sustain their long working hours.

Every morning. around 5 or 6am, they would get up and start work, either preparing the horses or milking the cows, then returning to the farm kitchen around 6 or 6.45 for their breakfasts. Most of the kitchens had a large cooking range at one end, and a long table, scrubbed white, along the window wall, with a bench down each side. Early in the nineteenth century the thick table tops were carved out to provide a series of plate-sized hollows about two inches deep into which the broth, meat and vegetables were poured before being eaten with wooden *gob-sticks,* as spoons were then known. The whole table was then washed down with hot water and soda, although in some houses wisps of straw were used for rough cleaning. By the 1850s these tables had been replaced by the usual plank-topped variety on which wooden trenchers (372-373) were laid for each person, the 1890s seeing these replaced in turn by white earthenware plates. Cutlery, however, could still remain quite rudimentary, some men using their clasp knives at table in preference to knives and forks. Even in the 1980s it was quite possible to be seated at a Moorland farm table set with only a single two-pronged fork, a plate of cold meat, a jar of pickles, and a plate in front of each person. The fork was used solely to transfer the meat and the pickles to the individual plates, each diner being expected to eat with his own clasp knife. This represents the height of polite manners of the early seventeenth century, but survived here unchanged for the next 350 years. At most farms, however, Sheffield knives and forks(387-437) were in regular use from at least the 1900s, these being arranged in a cross at the end of the meal, rather than side by side in the modern manner. This could be a Christian symbol, but in this region it is just as likely to signify a protection against witchcraft.[4]

Back in 1812, H.E.Strickland's *General View of the Agriculture of the East Riding of Yorkshire* recorded that breakfast and supper were virtually identical meals, comprising cold meat, fruit pies, cheesecakes and milk. A hundred and seventeen years later, Bert Frank, the founder of the Ryedale Folk Museum, received just the same meals when he started work around Gillamoor and Fadmoor.[5] Here the kitchen range was lit at 6am, so that water from the boiler would be ready for them to wash when they returned at 6.45. They then sat down to breakfast, the shepherd, who was also the foreman, taking the armchair at the head of the table, from where he carved two thick slices from a huge joint of cold fat boiled bacon. Afterwards everyone could help themselves to the foot-diameter apple, prune, jam or curd pies which had been placed on the table, one pie being finished before another was started. To cut his slice, he held the plate steady with two fingers on the edge of the crust, the first cut being made from the centre to the left side of the fingers, the second cut then being made from half an inch short of the centre to the right side of the fingers. Each succeeding cut was made in the same way, proceeding anti-clockwise around the pie, until the last piece was left with a hexagonal piece at the centre. This method ensured that everyone had the same amount of crust to filling, and also that no-one ever handled anyone else's piece of pie.[18] A pile of split and buttered sad-cake, or plain turf-cake, could then be spread with jam, or more probably with Golden Syrup, to complete breakfast, bread not being eaten here to any great extent. After feeding the stock, and other farm work, dinner was served at mid-day. The first course was rice pudding, the sweet always being served first here, then came the Yorkshire Pudding, served in the traditional manner in large squares, as a course in its own right. The plate, for the same one was used throughout the meal, was then heaped high with slices of roast beef and vegetables, the hungry lads eating every morsel. After working throughout the afternoon, supper was served in the early evening, its contents being virtually the same as those which appeared at breakfast.

For the women of the house, satisfying this continuous demand for food meant that much of their time was spent in the kitchen, constantly roasting, boiling, baking and preserving, for everything was made from raw materials, convenience foods hardly ever being used here. To start the day, the first task was to light the kitchen fire and its adjoining oven, to ensure that they could provide sufficient heat for cooking. Since breakfast was largely a cold meal, except for heating the milk for the men's basins, it was quickly prepared simply by bringing out the required food from the pantry, and setting it out on the table.

After pig-killing, the sides of bacon had been scalded, scraped,and laid down on a clean paved or cement floor in a cool part of the house, and then sprinkled with salt and saltpetre and left for two or three weeks, more being added if it was all absorbed. After this time it was washed clean, and hung up to dry ready for use. As for the hams, they were cured either in an identical manner, or by using recipes such as the following example from the Healey recipe book;

'To Cure Hams

For two large Hams, one lb.,two and a half oz. of common salt, two and a half oz. of saltpetre, three oz. of bay salt, one lb. of coarse sugar. boil them together in a quart of stale strong beer. When the pickle is cold rub the Hams with it every day, for 16 days altogether. Hang them up in a chimney where wood is burnt. The saltpetre and bay salt must be powdered. Throw the liquor over the top of the Hams. They must be soaked two nights and a day in cold water before they are boiled for use. Never cure Hams later than Feb. 7th. Keep them in pickle six weeks before you hang them up to dry'.

Even today numerous houses have damp patches on their floors, or areas where salt crystals still emerge in damp weather, showing where curing took place many years ago. Other pork products made after pig-killing included black puddings, chitterlings, sausages, pork pies, lard (and its crispy by-product 'scrappings'), and brawns. David Wood, who grew up at Holly Park, a farm near Kirkby Moorside, where their big bacon pigs got up to 40 stone, can remember how these were made.

Four pig's feet and the pig's head, prepared by being split in two, and having the lower jaw, cheeks, eyes, brains and inner ears removed, were put into brine for a week, and then taken out and allowed to dry. They were next boiled in a big jam pan or an outside copper with two pounds of shin-beef to make it firm (some farms using an old hen for this purpose), salt, pepper, and just sufficient water, until the meat was so soft that it fell to pieces when stirred with a spoon. After leaving it to become cold, all the bones were picked out, and the meat and juices thoroughly mixed together with the hands, working up to the elbows in the mixture. A layer of this brawn was then put into the bottom of a pot, a freshly-cooked pig's tongue curled on top, and then the pot filled up with more of the brawn, after which it was left to set. When cold, it could be turned out, and served at the table in thick slices.

 Most pork products were home-made in this way, but there were good pork butchers too, as well as a number of professional bacon-curers in the area, such as Simpsons of Gillamoor, or Inman Brothers of Norton, who sold their products both locally, and to customers as far away as London. When required for breakfast, a large joint of the thick, fat bacon was cut off the flitch, and soaked in cold water for an hour or two, or longer, to remove some of the excess salt. After being scraped to remove any 'rusty' or other unsound areas, it was placed in a pot of fresh cold water, brought up to the boil, and simmered until tender, about an hour and a half for a two pound (1kg) joint. It was then taken out, trimmed and the rind removed, the whole then being sprinkled with dried breadcrumbs or grated crust, and perhaps dried off before the fire for a few minutes before being put into the pantry to cool, ready for breakfast next day.

As for the pies, these were made in broad pie plates about a foot (30cm) in diameter.

Fruit Pies

Pastry; 450g (1 lb) plain flour   100g (4oz) lard
*   2.5ml (½ tsp) salt   90-120 ml (6-8 tbs) water*

1. sprinkle the salt into the flour, add the lard in small lumps, and rub it in until the mixture resembles fine breadcrumbs
2. sprinkle on the water, stirring it in with a round-bladed knife, then lightly knead to form a smooth dough.
3. divide the dough into two, roll out one piece about a foot in diameter on a floured board, and then do the same with the other
4. line the pie dish with one piece of the pastry, then fill it with either;
*   1350-1575g (3-3½ lb) of cooking apples, peeled, cored and sliced,*
*   with 100g (4oz) sugar or 1350g (3lb) of topped & tailed gooseberries, or*
*   rhubarb cut in 2.5cm (1 inch) lengths, with 225g (8oz) sugar or 675g (1½ lb)*
*   pitted prunes, scalded with water or tea, left to soak overnight, with 75g*
*   (3 oz) sugar*
5. damp the edges, put on the lid, trim the edges, and use the trimmings as decoration and to form a circle around a central vent-hole, then bake at 200°C, 400°F, gas mark 6 for 40-45 minutes.

Once breakfast had been cleared, it was already time to start preparing for the mid-day dinner, making sure that all the roast and boiled meats would be ready on time, along with the vegetables and the Yorkshire Pudding.

Yorkshire Pudding

100g (4oz) plain flour   275ml (½pt) mixed milk and water
2 eggs   dripping
pinch of salt

1. mix the flour and salt in a basin, make a hole in the centre, break in the eggs, and gradually add the milk and water, beating the mixture continuously to absorb the flour from the sides, and produce a smooth batter
2. leave the batter to stand for at least 30 min.
3. put a little dripping in a dripping pan, place in an oven pre-heated to 200°C, 400°F, gas mark 6, until it is smoking hot
4. Pour in the batter, and bake for 30 min. until crisp and brown. Cut in squares and serve immediately with good brown gravy

Alternatively the Yorkshire pudding could be made with beastings, the first or second milking after a cow had calved. Being extremely rich, the beastings were usually portioned out amongst favoured neighbours for making custards etc. They were very careful to make sure that the vessel containing the beastings was never washed out before being returned, since this was very unlucky, and would probably cause the death of the new calf.[6]

Beastings Yorkshire Pudding[7]

225ml (8fl oz) beastings   2.5ml (½ tsp) salt
100g (4oz) flour   cold water

1. make up the batter as above, adding sufficient water until the batter runs easily from the spoon, and bake as a normal Yorkshire pudding

As an alternative, especially if a pork joint was being roasted, a savoury or seasoned pudding would be made;

Savoury Pudding, Miss Crosland

100g (4oz) suet *100g (4oz) flour*
225g (8oz) fresh breadcrumbs *salt & pepper*
100g (4oz) finely chopped onions *milk*
1 egg, beaten *(15ml [1tbs] each of sage & marjoram)*
1. mix the dry ingredients and stir in the egg and sufficient milk to form a soft dough
2. fork the mixture level in a greased dripping tin, and bake at 200°C, 400°F, gas mark 6 for about 30 minutes until crisp and brown on the top

As for the joints of meat, instead of being roasted, the coarser cuts were usually stewed to make the meat tender, and to retain the flavour. The traditional method was simply to roll the meat in a mixture of flour, salt and pepper, and then stew it in water for four to five hours, but there were also richer versions, such as the following, which probably dates from the late eighteenth century;

To Stew Beef Mrs L.Hartley

900g (2lb) braising steak, cut into cubes *pepper & salt*
900g (2lb) onions, peeled, halved and sliced
450g (1lb) each of carrots, turnips and quartered onions prepared for boiling
1. pack alternate layers of the steak and of the sliced onions inside a deep casserole, adding pepper and salt to taste as it is filled
2. pour in water to three parts fill the casserole, seal the top with kitchen foil, and bake at 170°C, 325°F, gas mark 3, for three hours
3. 30 min. before the beef is done, put the remaining vegetables into a pan with a little salt, cover them with water, and simmer them for 15-20 minutes until cooked
4. to serve, either drain the vegetables and tip them on top of the stew in the casserole, or pour the stew into a large tureen, and cover it with the vegetables

Today, joints of meat are hardly ever pickled and boiled in Ryedale, but for centuries, up to around the 1940s and '50s, boiling was the most common method. If carefully done, even the coarser joints could be made tender and flavoursome. Perhaps more importantly, very little of their nutritional value was lost, for all their juices were retained in the water in which they were cooked, rather than being evaporated or lost into the dripping pan, as happened when meat was being roasted.
In this region, the beef was traditionally wet-salted in brine, both to flavour it, and to preserve it. Miss Crosland's recipe is typical;

Salt or Corned Beef

4.5kg (10lb) beef, such as brisket *10g (¹/₂oz) Bay salt (coarse sea salt)*
75g (3oz) saltpetre *450g (1 lb) coarse brown sugar*
675g (1 lb 8oz) common salt *4.6 litres (8pt) hot water*
1. put all the salts and the sugar into a large pot, and scald with the hot water. Stir it, and leave it until all has dissolved and it is quite cold
2. put in the beef, ensuring that it is covered, and leave it for 2 to 3 days, turning it every day, if it is required for use at that time. For long-term preservation it must be kept in the

pickle for at least two weeks, the Healey recipe book stating that it 'will keep in this pickle two or three months'
3. remove the beef from the pickle, soak it in cold water for a few hours if it has been in the pickle for a long time, then roll it tightly, securing it with string or tape, then roll it in flour
4. Bring a large pot of fresh water up to a fast boil, put in the beef, then reduce the heat to a very gentle simmer, and continue cooking it for about 5 hours. It may then be served hot,(in which case sliced carrots, parsnips etc. may be added 30 min before serving) or pressed under a heavy weight and be sliced thinly when cold

Fresh meat also ate well when rolled and stewed, as in G. Yeoman's recipe;

Beef Roll

900g (2lb) braising steak, in 1 or 2 pieces, cut about 1.5cm ($^1/_2$inch) thick
100g (4oz) ham or tongue   2 eggs, beaten
100g (4oz) fresh white breadcrumbs   salt & pepper to taste
15ml (1 tbs) flour
1. finely chop or mince the ham or tongue, mix with the breadcrumbs, salt and pepper, then mix in the eggs to form a stuffing
2. trim the steaks, lightly beat them with a rolling pin, lay them out as a large rectangle, spread the stuffing over them, roll them up like a Swiss roll, and truss them with either string or tapes
3. Place the roll in a pie dish, pour in 425ml ($^3/_4$pt) boiling water, cover it over with kitchen foil, and bake at 180°C, 350°F, gas mark 4 for 2-2$^1/_2$ hours
4. Lift the roll onto a hot dish. Mix the flour with 60ml (4tbs) cold water in a saucepan, pour in the stock from the pie dish, then heat it, stirring continuously, until it simmers. Add salt and pepper to taste, pour it over the beef roll, and serve. The roll also carves well when cold

Although no longer to be found in Ryedale butcher's shops, the following dish is still sold in Todmorden Market Hall in the West Riding, thinly sliced either for sandwiches or as a substitute for slices of roast beef.

Beef Mould, Miss Crosland

450g (1 lb) shin or stewing beef, trimmed and cut into small cubes
575ml (1 pt) water   5ml (1 tsp) copped sage, parsley & thyme
5ml (1 tsp) salt   30ml (2 tbs) gelatin
pinch of black pepper   2.5ml ($^1/_2$tsp) anchovy sauce
1. put the beef, cold water, salt, pepper and herbs into a saucepan, and leave to soak for about an hour
2. cover the pan, and heat it gently to stew the meat very slowly for 4 to 5 hours, for it is important not to waste any of the gravy through evaporation
3. mix 75ml (5 tbs) cold water with the gelatin in a cup, pour in some of the gravy from the meat, stir it until it has completely dissolved, and then return it to the meat. Add the anchovy sauce, and stir it in thoroughly
4. rinse a pudding basin with cold water, pour in the meat, leave it in a cool place overnight to set, then turn it out onto a plate and slice thinly

To accompany the cold meat, large jars of pickled onions and pickled red cabbage were prepared every year;

Pickled Red Cabbage[8]

1 red cabbage	*around 100g (4oz) salt*
575ml (1 pt) vinegar	*5ml (1 tsp) mustard powder*
25g (1 oz) pickling spice	

1. cut the cabbage vertically into four, cut out the white stalk, and slice the remainder into shreds
2. lay the cabbage on a flat dish and sprinkle it with the salt. Leave it 24 hours for a crisp pickle, but for a more tender pickle, let it lie 5 days, stirring it every day and adding a little more salt
3. pack the cabbage into jars
4. boil the vinegar with the spices for 5 min., stir in the mustard, allow it to cool, and when cold pour it over the cabbage, and seal the jars

The meat was accompanied by potatoes and vegetables, the latter either being cooked in a bag of netted string plunged into an iron pot, or cooked in a stewpan. Then came more fruit pies, and the hot puddings, which were either boiled in the pot, or baked in the oven. Some of the boiled puddings contained excessive amounts of suet, one of Jane Trenham's treacle puddings actually having more suet than flour, but others were much more palatable;

Boiled Fruit Pudding, Miss Crosland

225g (8 oz) plain flour	*about 150ml ($^{1}/_{4}$ pt)*
75g (3 oz) suet	*30ml (2 tbs) sugar*
5ml (1 tsp) baking powder	*450g (1 lb) cooking apples or soft fruit*

1. peel, core, and coarsely chop the apples
2. mix the flour, suet and baking powder in a bowl, use a round-bladed knife to stir in enough water to form a soft dough, and knead it very lightly until smooth
3. cut off a third of the pastry, roll it out, and use it to line a greased 1200ml (2 pt) pudding basin, fill this with the apples sprinkled with the sugar, damp the edges, then roll out the remaining pastry to form a lid, and put it in place, pressing the edges to form a neat joint all round
4. cut a piece of greaseproof paper and a piece of kitchen foil large enough to cover the basin, fold a pleat across their centre, and put them on top of the pudding, greaseproof-side down, then tie them in place with string, leaving enough to tie across the pudding to form a handle
5. steam the pudding for around two hours. Alternatively a traditional round pudding can be formed in a cloth resting within the basin, the cloth then being tightly tied over the pudding, lifted out of the basin, plunged into boiling water and cooked for the same time

Ginger Pudding, Jane Trenham

100g (4 oz) flour	*75g (3 oz) suet*
100g (4 oz) fresh breadcrumbs	*1 egg, beaten*
2.5ml ($^{1}/_{2}$ tsp) ground ginger	*5ml (1 tsp) baking powder*
50g (2 oz) sugar	*45ml (3 tbs) golden syrup, warmed*
110ml (4 fl. oz) milk	*2.5ml ($^{1}/_{2}$ tsp) bicarbonate of soda*

1. mix all the dry ingredients in a basin
2. beat the egg into the milk, and stir these, with the treacle, into the other ingredients
3. grease a 1200ml (2 pt) pudding basin, put in the mixture, seal it with greaseproof paper and foil, as in the last recipe, and steam for 2 hours

Apple Crumb Pudding, Jane Trenham
675g (1½ lb) cooking apples, peeled, cored & sliced
150g (6 oz) fresh white breadcrumbs   *10ml (2 tsp) ground cinnamon*
75g (3 oz) butter   *125g (5 oz) sugar*
1. grease a pt. ceramic baking or souffle dish
2. put in a quarter of the breadcrumbs and dot with a quarter of the butter, cut in small lumps
3. add a third of the apples, sprinkled with a third of the sugar and cinnamon, then alternate layers of breadcrumbs and apples to fill the dish
4. bake in a pre-heated oven at 1800C, 350°F, gas mark 4 for 45-60 minutes

Before the days when Goodall and Backhouse and similar companies introduced their cornflour-based custard powders, the puddings were accompanied by sauces such as sugar, butter and nutmeg, melted together and served hot, or by real custard sauces, such as Jane Trenham's version;

Custard
600ml (1 pt) milk   *2 or 3 eggs, beaten*
2 bayleaves   *30 to 45ml (2 to 3 tbs) sugar*
1 stick of cinnamon
1. bring the milk, bayleaves and cinnamon up to the boil, and let it stand for 15 min.
2. strain the eggs into a jug, stir in the sugar, and then pour in the milk, while stirring
3. put the jug in a saucepan of water boiling on the stove, and continue stirring until the custard has thickened, then either serve immediately, or pour it into a cold jug to prevent it from continuing to cook to a solid curd

In addition to cooking for the usual breakfasts, dinners and suppers, the women of the farm also had to prepare the additional meals required for harvest, for threshing days, or for clipping days, when there would be many more hungry mouths to feed. For most of these meals it would be a case of making larger quantities of the dishes regularly served in the farm kitchen, but some additional things were also prepared to be carried out to the fields. Among these were ham or bacon cakes;

Ham Cake
1 large slice of gammon   *100g (2 oz) lard*
100g (4 oz) plain flour   *20ml (4 tsp) water*
pinch of salt
1. rub the lard into the flour and salt, mix in the water to form short pastry, and roll this out on a floured board
2. trim the gammon and remove the rind, lay it on one end of the pastry, damp the edges, fold the remaining pastry over the gammon, and seal it to form a pasty
3. Prick the top with a fork, place on a baking sheet, and bake at 220°C, 425°F, gas mark 7 for 15 min., then reduce the temperature to 170°C, 325°F, gas mark 3 for a further 30 min.

These, together with perhaps currant pasty, buttered sad cake, bread and cheese, etc. were washed down with a variety of drinks, such as beer or herbal beers (326-337), cold tea, or one of the traditional harvest drinks such as the following example, which was made fresh daily;

Gale Beer (Bert Frank's mother's recipe, Hutton le Hole)

10-12 sprigs fresh young gale (bog myrtle,or Sweet Gale, Myrica gale)
225g (8 oz) sugar   *12.5g ($^1\!/_2$ oz) yeast*
5 litres (8 pt) boiling water
1. pour the boiling water onto the gale and sugar, leave until it has cooled to blood heat, then add the yeast
2. leave overnight in a warm place, then bottle and cork lightly
3. although not originally used, a sliced lemon could be added to the gale and sugar

Gale Beer

a fistfull of gale   *5 litres (8 pt) boiling water*
450g (1 lb) moist sugar   *12.5g ($^1\!/_2$ oz) yeast*
12.5g ($^1\!/_2$ oz) root ginger, bruised   *a slice of toast*
1. scald the gale,sugar and ginger with the boiling water, allow to cool to blood heat, spread with yeast on top of the toast, float this on the liquid, leave overnight in a warm place, then bottle and cork lightly

Elderflower Champagne

4 heads elderflower   *5 litres (8 pt) boiling water*
675g (1$^1\!/_2$ lb) sugar   *2 lemons*
30ml (2 tbs) white wine vinegar
1. squeeze the lemons, quarter them, and put the juice and peels with the other ingredients into a large bowl
2. stand for 24 hours, stirring occasionally, then strain it into bottles and cork lightly
3. leave for a few days before drinking

Ginger Beer, G. Yeoman's

25g (1 oz) root ginger, bruised   *1 lemon*
600ml (1 lb) brown sugar   *25g (1 oz) yeast*
5 litres (8 pt) boiling water
1. bruise the root ginger, pare the yellow zest from the lemon, and squeeze out and strain the juice
2. put the sugar, ginger, lemon zest and juice into a large vessel, pour on the water, and leave until cooled to blood heat
3. stir in the yeast, cover the vessel, and leave in a warm place overnight
4. strain into bottles, cork lightly, and keep in a cool place for a few days, when it will be ready to drink.

The kitchen of Poverty Hill Farm, Rudland, in 1934. The squab, an upholstered bench, and the tripod table, are typical pieces of farmhouse furniture. The foreman and other farm servants would take their meals at a long wooden table, probably lined with benches, along the window side of the room. Note the range, with its brightly polished crane and reckons, and the tap fitted to the L-shaped boiler.

Teatime Recipes

In a county famed for its home baking, it is not surprising that all the recipe books in the Ryedale Folk Museum include dozens of recipes for the cakes, biscuits, and other sweet dishes which were served at tea-time, especially on Sunday afternoons, or whenever visitors were received. Cottagers, farmer's wives and the housekeepers in the largest houses made a very similar range of bakery. This is to be expected, since the whole tradition of fine home bakery started in the country house and vicarage, the girls trained there then continuing to use the same recipes, perhaps a little more economically, when they left to set up their own homes. Starting with the cakes, most were raised with eggs, but from the mid nineteenth century the use of sodium bicarbonate, cream of tartar and baking powders became widespread, since these greatly assisted the cakes to rise successfully.

A Cake, Mrs Gill

175g (6 oz) plain flour	*100g (4 oz) currants*
175g (6 oz) sugar	*10ml (2 tsp) brandy*
3 eggs, less one white	*175g (6 oz) butter*

1. cream the butter with the sugar until light and fluffy, then mix in the eggs and brandy, a little at a time, beating well after each addition. Fold in the currants, and then the flour
2. line an 18cm (7 inch) round tin with greased greaseproof paper, pour in the mixture, and bake at 170°C, 325°F, gas mark 3, for 1¹/₂ hours

A Cake for Common Use, Jane Trenham

225g (8 oz) sugar	*2 eggs, beaten*
100g (4 oz) butter	*100g (4 oz) chopped candied peel*
25g (1 oz) lard	*12.5g (¹/₂ tsp) grated nutmeg*
225g (8 oz) flour	*30ml (2 tbs) brandy*

1. cream the butter and lard with the sugar, then beat in the eggs and brandy, little by little, to form a smooth mixture. Fold in the candied peel, then the flour and nutmeg
2. grease an 18cm (7 inch) round cake tin, pour in the mixture, and bake at 180C, 350F, gas mark 4 for around 1¹/₂ hours

Sultana Cake, C.A.Yeoman's

150g (6 oz) butter or lard	*50g (2 oz) sultanas & candied peel, or*
150g (6 oz) sugar	*more to taste*
1 egg, beaten	*275g (10 oz) flour*
200ml (7 fl. oz) milk	*5ml (1 tsp) baking powder*

1. cream the butter or lard with the sugar, beat in the egg, then the milk, then the sultanas and peel, and finally fold in the flour mixed with the baking powder
2. bake in a greased and lined 18 cm (7 inch) round cake tin at 180°C, 350°F, gas mark 4 for 1¹/₂ hours

Walnut Bread (sent from Sophia Blakey's house to Miss Crosland, August, 1924)

This bread is not as sweet as cake, and is best served sliced and buttered.

225g (8 oz) flour	*30ml (2 tbs) golden syrup*
50g (2 oz) cornflour	*10ml (2 tsp) baking powder*
60ml (2 tbs) sugar	*1 egg, beaten*
50g (2 oz) chopped walnuts	*300ml (¹/₂ pt) milk*

1. line a large loaf tin with greased greaseproof paper
2. mix all the dry ingredients in a bowl, make a well in the centre, pour in the egg, with a little of the milk, then stirring them, gradually working in the flour etc., and the rest of the milk, to form a soft mixture
3. place the mixture in the loaf tin, and bake at 180C, 350F, gas mark 4, for 1½ hours

One of the great tea-time specialities of this region was the cheesecake, an individual tart with a short pastry base filled with a variety if ingredients, rather than the stodgy, smooth textured, biscuit-based slab American-style cheesecake found in today's supermarkets and restaurants. The original cheesecake was probably the kind made with curds extracted from skim milk in most Yorkshire dairies. It could still be bought recently on market stalls, often being brought there in large rectangular enamel bread pots, and is commercially manufactured and packed by dairies such as Langley Farm, Holmfirth, West Yorkshire.

All the following recipes require 225g (8 oz) shortcrust pastry, rolled out and used to line large tart tins, and are baked at 200°C, 400°F, gas mark 6, for 10 minutes, then reducing the temperature to 180C, 350F, gas mark 4 for a further 20 minutes

Curd Cheesecakes

225g (8 oz) curd	*50g (2 oz) currants*
2 eggs, beaten	*30ml (2 tbs) double cream*
100g (4 oz) melted butter	*12.5 (½ tsp) grated nutmeg, or to taste*
100g (4 oz) sugar	*grated peel of 1 lemon (optional)*

Mix all the ingredients together, fill the cases, and bake

Egg Cheesecakes, Jane Trenham

2 hard-boiled eggs, chopped fine	*100g (4 oz) currants*
100g (4 oz) butter	*15ml (1 tbs) cream*
100g (4 oz) sugar	*15ml (1 tbs) brandy*
1 raw egg	

cream the butter and the sugar, beat in the egg, mix in the cream and brandy, then the chopped eggs and currants, half fill the cases, and bake

Rice Cheesecakes, Jane Trenham

100g (4 oz) butter	*2 eggs*
100g (4 oz) sugar	*juice & grated rind of a lemon*
50g (2 oz) ground rice	

cream the butter and the sugar, beat in the eggs, then the lemon juice and rind, and the ground rice, half fill the cases and bake

Potato Cheesecakes, Mrs L.Hartley

150g (3 oz) butter	*juice & grated rind of a lemon*
150g (3 oz) sugar	*3 eggs*
225g (8 oz) mashed potato	

cream the butter and the sugar, beat in the eggs, then the remaining ingredients, half-fill the cases, and bake

Apple Cheesecakes, Mrs Leighton

100g (4 oz) butter	*4 egg yolks*
125g (5 oz) sugar	*5 ml (1 tsp) lemon juice*
225g (8 oz) grated eating apple	*pinch grated nutmeg*

cream the butter with the sugar, beat in the egg yolks, then the remaining ingredients, half-fill the cases, and bake

Lemon cheesecakes were popular too, these being made with lemon cheese or lemon curd, a rich blend of lemons, egg yolks and sugar which could be sealed into jars, like jam, ready for use at any time. As well as making good cheesecakes, it is delicious when simply spread on bread and butter, or on scones.

Lemon Cheesecakes, (Healey), smooth, with a sharper flavour

150g (6 oz) butter	*4 lemons*
150g (6 oz) lump sugar	*6 egg yolks*

1. rub the lumps of sugar on the lemon rind to extract the yellow zest
2. melt the butter in a saucepan, stir in the sugar, then the strained lemon juice, and finally the beaten egg yolks
3. stir the mixture over a gentle heat until it forms a thick yellow jam, then either pour it into sterilised jars and seal down for future use, or use fresh
4. line individual tart tins with 225g (8 oz) shortcrust pastry, and bake these blind at 200C, 400F, gas mark 6 for 10-15 minutes, until set. Remove the cases from the oven, fill them with the lemon cheese, then replace them in the oven for a few minutes to set

Lemon Cheesecakes, (Jane Trenham), slightly textured, with a mellow flavour

3 lemons	*15ml (1tbs) ground almonds*
225g (8 oz) butter	*4 eggs, beaten*
225g (8 oz) sugar	

1. grate the rind from the lemons and put them in a saucepan with their strained juice
2. add the remainder of the ingredients, and simmer them gently, stirring continuously until, as the original says, it has 'the consistency of honey', then either seal in sterilised jars, or use fresh
3. bake as in the recipe above

Moving on to biscuits, most of these were made from a soft dough, lumps of which were dropped on to the baking sheet, where they spread out as shallow domes of crisp biscuit. For brandy-snaps, the dough spread out so thinly that it actually boiled on the baking sheet, then, on being taken from the oven, it was rolled around the handles of wooden spoons to achieve its traditional cylindrical shape.

Sweet Biscuits, Mrs Pearse

100g (4 oz) plain flour	*1 egg, beaten*
100g (4 oz) sugar	*150ml (¹/₄ pt) milk*
100g (4 oz) currants	

1. mix the dry ingredients, make a hole in the centre, drop in the egg, gradually working it in with just sufficient milk to produce a soft dropping consistency
2. spoon walnut-sized lumps 8cm (3 inches) apart on a greased baking sheet and bake for about 20 minutes at 150°C, 300°F, gas mark 2, until lightly coloured, just browning at the edges

Seed Biscuits, Jane Trenham

100g (4 oz) plain flour	2 eggs beaten
100g (4 oz) butter	5ml(1 tsp) carraway seed
100g (4 oz) sugar	

1. rub the butter into the flour, stir in the carraway seed, and mix in the egg to form a soft paste
2. bake as in the recipe above

Gingerbread (biscuits), Mrs St.A.Warde

100g (4 oz) treacle	2.5ml ($^{1}/_{2}$ tsp)each, ground cinnamon & cloves
100g (4 oz) sugar	5ml (1 tsp) each of carraway seeds & ginger
100g (4 oz) butter	275g (10 oz) flour

1. place a saucepan on the scales and weigh in the treacle, then add the sugar, spices and butter, and heat gently, stirring continuously until the butter has completely melted, then allow it to cool
2. work in the flour, little by little, until it forms a stiff dough
3. knead well, roll into small balls the size of walnuts, place 8cm (3 inches) apart on greased baking sheets, and bake at 150C, 300F, gas mark 2, for 15-20 minutes

Very crisp when baked, these nuts soon become soft enough for eating after being left for a few days in the kitchen, or a slightly damp pantry. Airtight tins were not in use when this recipe was written around 1800.

Hunting Nuts (Brandy Snaps) Jane Trenham

75g (3 oz) flour	75g (3 oz) golden syrup (or black treacle for
75g (3 oz) sugar	dark, toffee-flavoured snaps
75g (3 oz) butter	10ml (2 tsp) ground ginger

1. rub the butter into the flour and ginger, rub in the sugar, then make a hole in the centre of the mixture, place the bowl on the scales and weigh in the warmed syrup/treacle, then stir together to form a stiff paste
2. spoon large walnut-sized lumps of the mixture about 100-125cm (4-5 inches) apart on greased baking sheets and bake at 180°F 350°C, gas mark 4 for about 10 minutes
3. when the biscuits have spread out to a thin, bubbling sheet, remove the baking sheet from the oven, allow it to cool a little, then roll each one around the handle of a wooden spoon. Allow to set, then slip them off and store in an airtight tin to keep them crisp

Other dishes to appear at tea-time could include a range of cold meats, etc., sandwiches, jams, jellies or honey to be spread on buttered bread, scones or turf-cakes, and perhaps preserved or bottled fruit, eaten with cream, and accompanied by more bread and butter. There may also be moulded jellies or creams, such as Jane Trenham's custard mould, or her rich trifle;

Custard Mould

20ml (4 tsp) gelatin	2 bay leaves
150ml ($^{1}/_{4}$ pt) cold water	4 egg yolks
600ml (1pt) milk	

1. put the gelatin in a basin, and mix with the cold water
2. pour the milk into a saucepan with the bay leaves, bring to the boil, remove from the heat, and allow it to cool for 5 minutes, then pour it over the gelatin, stirring it until it has

all dissolved, then return the mixture to the saucepan, and leave it until cool

3. beat up the egg yolks, stir them into the mixture, and heat it up, stirring continuously until it has thickened like a custard, but do not allow it to boil, then dip the pan in cold water to prevent the mixture from cooking any further

4. pour the mixture immediately into a freshly-rinsed basin or mould, and leave in a cold place to set

This smooth, bland mould eats well with either cold stewed (tinned) fruit, or with jam

Trifle

1 pack trifle sponges, or stale spongecake	*1 pint pack custard powder*
100g (4 oz) macaroons	*5ml (1 tsp) lemon essence*
50g (2 oz) nibbed/finely chopped blanched almonds	*2 egg whites (use sterilised egg whites since they will not be cooked)*
450g (1 lb) jar raspberry jam	*60ml (4 tbs) sugar*
100ml (4 fl. oz) or to taste, sherry	*red food colouring*

1. take a large glass dish, and fill it with alternate layers of the sliced sponges and the macaroons, putting a layer of almonds and raspberry jam, between each layer

2. pour the sherry over the top, to give as even a soaking as possible, then leave the trifle overnight

3. mix the custard powder in a bowl with 45ml (3 tbs) of the sugar and 150ml (1/4 pt) of the milk. Bring the remainder of the milk to the boil, pour it into the custard powder mixture, while stirring, return to the saucepan, and bring it slowly to the boil, stirring continuously until smooth and thick, then pour it over the trifle, and allow it to cool

4. make up the sterilised egg whites, beat them to a very firm froth, and pipe them over the cold custard

5. place the remaining 15ml (1 tbs) sugar into a bowl, add 1 or 2 drops of red food colouring, and stir it to give the sugar a pink colour. Sprinkle this on top of the trifle just before it is served

Turf cakes were a speciality of the Wagon and Horses Inn at Saltersgate, where they were baked in one of the locally-made ovens. For making the tea, three kettles swing from the chimney crane, two more simmer on the turf-plate, and another stands ready nearby.

Country House Food

All the food served in English country houses during the Victorian and Edwardian periods was of the very highest quality. The finest of ingredients were either grown on the home farms and in the kitchen gardens, or were imported from Britain's massive Empire. French chefs, English cooks trained in the Anglo-French tradition, and various housekeepers, stillroom maids, pastry cooks, vegetable maids, kitchen maids and scullery staff were all available to cook them to perfection, using the vast array of ranges, stoves, ovens and other more specialised equipment provided for this purpose. Given these sumptuous resources, no effort was spared in producing dishes in which every aspect of flavour, aroma, texture and colour was enhanced to achieve virtual perfection.

The following recipes come from two sources. The earliest, dating from around 1800, come from the recipe book used by the Healey/Hartley family of Middleton Lodge, the delightful house at Middleton Tyas built for them in the late eighteenth century by the great John Carr of York. The later examples come from the recipe book of Miss Helen Crosland, whose former home,'Elphield' is now part of the Ryedale Folk Museum. In 1895 she had attended the Sheffield School of Cookery and Domestic Training, where the principal, Ms M.O.Angwin, provided courses in 'Superior Cookery' of this kind. At this time the new 'service a' la Russe' had become fashionable, at which numerous courses of beautifully prepared and presented dishes were handed round the table by the footmen, each guest in turn helping themselves from the dishes. First came a choice of either clear or thick soup, then the fish, then the delicate entrees, perhaps moulded in little chicken moulds (85-86) or dariole moulds ((87-88). Then came the main meat course, which could include dishes such as these;

Grenadine de Boeuf, Miss Crosland

450g (1lb) beefsteak, about 2.5cm (1 inch) thick
225g (8 oz) fat bacon, cut thick
675g (1½ lb) carrot, turnip & onion
300ml (1pt) stock
2.5ml (½ tsp) salt

675g (1½lb) potatoes
1 egg, beaten
300ml (½ pt) fresh tomato
sauce (see below)
225g (8oz) peas

1. cut the vegetables in quarters, put in a saucepan with the stock, cover, and bring to the boil
2. meanwhile beat the steak lightly, trim it into neat rounds, and, using a larding needle, and working across the grain of the meat, insert narrow strips of the bacon into the steak in neat rows of alternating 3 and then 4 strips, each strip having a U-shape, with both its ends portruding above the steak
3. trim the ends of the bacon to an even height, then place the steaks on top of the vegetables, cover, and cook for about 30 min, basting frequently with the stock, but not allowing the steak to settle into the stock
4. boil the potatoes until tender, drain them, rub them through a sieve, beat in the salt and the egg, and fork it into the form of a circular border around a hot dish, and keep it hot
5. simmer the peas until tender
6. pre-heat the oven to 200°C, 400° F, gas mark 6, and when the steak is cooked, remove it from the pan, place it in a metal dish, and bake it for 5 min.
7. Remove the vegetables from the stock, skim the stock, and boil it rapidly to reduce it to a thick glaze
8. Heat the tomato sauce to a simmer
9. drain the peas, pour them into the centre of the potato border, remove the steaks from

the oven, brush them with the stock, arrange them around the potato border, and finally pour the tomato sauce into the dish just before serving

Tomato Sauce

450g (1 lb) tomatoes	salt & pepper
2 shallots	5ml (1 tsp) thyme and marjoram
25g (1 oz) butter	5ml (1 tsp) vinegar
50g (2oz) lean ham	

finely chop all the ingredients, fry them gently in the butter for 10-15 min., add the vinegar, and salt and pepper to taste, then rub them through a fine sieve. Thin with a little light stock if neccesary

Mutton Cutlets, Mrs Hartley

6 small mutton chops	5ml (1 tsp) thyme & marjoram
275ml (½ pt) single cream	900g (2 lb) turnips
salt & pepper	300ml (½ pt) rich brown gravy
50g (2 oz) butter	

1. trim most of the fat off the chops, and neatly scrape all the meat etc. from the ends of the bones
2. peel and chop the turnips, and boil them in salted water for 20-30 min. until tender
3. meanwhile dust the chops with pepper, salt and the herbs, fry them gently in the butter, finally adding the cream to the pan just before serving, to make a thick sauce
4. mash the turnips, adding more salt and pepper to taste, and fork them into a shallow cone on a hot plate, pour the gravy around them, then arrange the chops on the sides of the cone of turnips, pour the pan juices over them, and serve hot.

Beef to imitate Hare, Miss Crosland

900g (2lb) stewing beef, cubed	2.5ml (½ tsp) salt
15ml (1 tbs) brown sugar	1.25ml (¼ tsp) pepper
30ml (2 tbs) vinegar	50ml (2tsp) red currant jam or jelly
25g (1 oz) lard or dripping	5ml (1 tsp) flour
pinch of ground mace	5ml (1 tsp) very finely chopped onion
600ml (1 pt) water	

1. place the beef in a pottery dish, rub it with the sugar and vinegar, turning it and rubbing it each day for 2 to 3 days
2. put the beef in a casserole with all the other ingredients, cover, and bake at 170°C, 325°F, gas mark 3 for about 2½ hours

Scotch Collops White, Mrs L.Hartley

450g (1 lb) lean leg of lamb	30ml (2 tbs) mushroom ketchup
75g (3 oz) butter	pinch of mace and of cayenne pepper
15ml (1 tbs) flour	one egg yolk
2.5ml (½ tsp) lemon pickle	200ml (⅓ pt) single cream

1. slice the meat as thinly as possible, and gently fry in batches in 50g (2 oz) of the butter, tipping the meat and the gravy it produces into a second pan placed over a low heat, until it is all cooked
2. melt the remaining butter and flour in the first pan and make a roux, mix in the pickle, ketchup and spices, and the gravy drained from the meat, and cook gently, stirring, for 5 minutes

3. beat the egg yolk and cream together, stir it into the sauce, then add the meat, and stir it together until hot, but not boiling, before serving

By the late eighteenth century, the increasing trade with India had already brought curries into the country house kitchen. These recipes from around 1800 provide instructions for making a curry powder for general use, as well as specific details for making a chicken curry. Like most curries of this period, they rely largely on turmeric for their colour and flavour, and black pepper for their heat.

Currie Powder

75g (3 oz) turmeric	12g (½ oz) cummin seed
25g (1 oz) black pepper	12g (½ oz) corriander seed
7g (¼ oz) cardamom seed	7g (¼ oz) ginger

Grind all these together in a pestle and mortar, and store ready for use in a small stoppered jar

Receipt for a Curry, Mrs Darville

1 chicken	2.5ml (½ tsp) salt
1 clove of garlic, crushed	15ml (1 tbs) turmeric
1 large English onion	5ml (1 tsp) black pepper
75g (3 oz) butter	large pinch each of ground cardamom,
juice of half a lemon	cummin, corriander & ginger

1. bone the chicken, cut it in pieces as if for stewing, and rub it with the garlic, salt and spices mixed to a paste with a little water
2. melt the butter in a thick-bottomed pan, put in the onion and chicken, and gently stir-fry until thoroughly cooked
3. serve with boiled rice

After the meat courses, a variety of puddings were served, some, like the cheese pudding below, being savoury, while others were sweet. Today we would never think of using either potatoes or carrots in sweet puddings, but they do eat surprisingly well.

Cheese Pudding, Mrs L.Hartley

225g (8 oz) potatoes, boiled and mashed	3 eggs
100g (4 oz) finely grated cheese	pepper and salt to taste
75g (3 oz) butter	

1. work the butter into the potatoes, then the cheese and the eggs, and the salt and pepper, beating (or blending) the mixture until quite smooth
2. pour into a greased 1200ml (2 pt) souffle dish and bake in an oven pre-heated to 150°C, 300°F, gas mark 2, for 45 minutes. Serve this souffle immediately

Potato Pudding, Mrs L. Hartley

225g (8 oz) potatoes, boiled & mashed	3 eggs
100g (4 oz) butter	juice & grated rind of half a lemon
75g (3 oz) sugar	

Follow the method given in the recipe above

Carrot Pudding

225g (8 oz) fresh white bread crumbs
225g (8 oz) finely grated carrot
4 eggs

75g (3 oz) butter, melted
75g (3 oz) sugar
2.5ml (½ tsp) grated nutmeg

1. mix the dry ingredients together, add the melted butter and beaten eggs, and stir the mixture thoroughly
2. place the mixture in a 1200ml (2 pt) ovenproof dish, and bake at 170°C, 325°F, gas mark 3, for an hour

Cabinet Pudding, Miss Crosland

glace cherries & angelica for decoration
6 trifle sponges, or savoy biscuits
25g (1 oz) ratafias
25g (1 oz) sugar

4 eggs, separated
600ml (1 pt) milk
a few drops of vanilla essence

1. grease a 900ml (1½ pt) mould or basin, and decorate the bottom with halved cherries and angelica
2. cut the sponge cakes or biscuits into pieces, and fill the mould with these and the ratafias
3. beat 4 yolks and 2 whites of egg together, add the sugar and vanilla, then bring the milk almost to the boil, and pour it slowly into the eggs, while stirring continuously
4. pour the mixture onto the cakes, cover the mould with greaseproof paper, and steam it for 30-40 minutes
5. remove the mould from the steamer, make sure that the pudding is loose all round, then turn it out onto a dish, and serve either hot or cold.

Amber Pudding, Miss Crosland

6 large cooking apples
75g (3 oz) sugar
3 eggs, separated
30ml (2 tbs) flour
glace cherries and angelica for decoration

50g (2 oz) butter
225g (½ lb) puff or shortcrust pastry
1 lemon
75g (3 oz) caster sugar

1. peel and slice the apples, and stew them with half the butter, the 75g (3 oz) of sugar, and the pared rind and juice of the lemon
2. when cooked, rub the pulp through a sieve, and beat the egg yolks and flour into it
3. grease a large pie dish, line it half-way down with the pastry, rolling out the trimmings, cutting them into small discs, and place them, overlapping, around the rim, as a decorative border
4. pour in the apple pulp, and bake at 200°C, 400°F, gas mark 6 for 30 to 35 min.
5. whisk the egg whites until stiff, whisk in half the caster sugar, fold in the remaining sugar, and pipe the meringue on top of the apple, then decorating it with the cherries and angelica
6. bake at 150°C, 300°F, gas mark 2 for 10 minutes, and serve either hot or cold

After the puddings, came the dessert, based on home-made ice-creams, a wide range of fruits grown in the hot-houses in the kitchen garden, both English and imported nuts, and perhaps a selection of pastries and cold sweets, such as;

Amber Tarts, Miss Crosland

1 tin apricot halves
1 egg yolk and 2 whites

225g (8 oz) flour
100g (4 oz) butter

50g (2 oz) caster sugar   5ml (1tsp) baking powder
glace cherries for decoration
1. sift the baking powder into the flour, rub in the butter, mix in the egg yolk and sufficient cold water to form a firm dough
2. roll out the pastry, cut it in circles, and use to line large tart tins. Bake these blind at 200°C, 400°F, gas mark 6, for 10-15 min.
3. place a half apricot in each tart, whisk the egg white and caster sugar to form a meringue, pipe this in a spiral to cover the apricot, place a cherry on top, and bake at 150°C, 300°F, gas mark 2, for 10 min.

Truffle of Apples, Mrs Oliver

225g (8 oz) pudding rice   600ml (1 pt) custard
peeled zest of a lemon or a stick of cinnamon   275ml ($^1/_2$ pt) whipped cream
6 eating apples, peeled and cored(not sliced)   125g (4 oz) sugar
1. gently simmer the rice with the zest or the cinnamon in 1.1 litres (2 pts) water in a covered pan for some 30 to 40 minutes, stirring continuously towards the end until it is very stiff
2. remove the zest or cinnamon, and model the rice as a 6cm (2 to 3 inch) high wall just inside the rim of a large dinner plate
3. meanwhile simmer the apples with the sugar and their peels in water for 10 to 15 minutes, until tender
4. drain the apples, arrange them within the rice wall, cover them with warm custard, and leave them to cool
5. pipe on the whipped cream, and serve

Stone Cream, Miss M.A.Lloyd

275ml (1 pt) double cream   1 small tin apricot halves, drained
30ml (2 tbs) caster sugar   grated rind, and juice of 1 lemon
10ml (2 tsp) gelatin
1. put the grated lemon rind and the juice into a shallow ceramic bowl, and arrange the apricots on top
2. melt the gelatin in 30ml (2tbs) boiling water in a cup, and then stand the cup in boiling water for a few minutes until completely dissolved. Gently beat the sugar into the cream, then mix in the gelatin, and pour over the apricots etc. in the bowl
3. leave in a cool place to set for a few hours. It may be served either sprinkled with sugar, or topped with a layer of sieved apricot jam

To make a Syllabub, Mrs L.Hartley

200ml (7 fl. oz) whipping cream   1 egg white(use sterilised egg white,
280ml ($^1/_2$ pt) red or white wine   since it will not be cooked)
1. share the wine out between 6 balloon wineglasses
2. whip the cream and the egg white together until thick, then carefully spoon it on top of the wine
3. leave for at least an hour in a cool place before serving

Jellies also appeared with the dessert, the finest being served in small, vertical jelly glasses, set out on elegant glass stands, and garnished with vine leaves. Compared to the larger moulded jellies, they had much richer and more intense flavours.

Port Wine Jelly, (Healey)

300ml (¹/₂ pt) port   *12ml (2¹/₂ tsp) gelatin*
50g (2 oz) sugar
1. put the gelatin, then the sugar, then the port, into a large jam jar, seal it with a piece of kitchen foil, stand the jar half its height in cold water in a saucepan, bring the water to the boil, and simmer gently for a further 10-15 minutes, until the sugar and gelatin have dissolved
2. stir the contents, replace the foil, allow to cool for 10 minutes, then pour into jelly or sherry glasses

Lemon Jelly, Mrs Hartley

150ml (¹/₄ pt)   strained lemon juice   *75g (3 oz) sugar*
1 egg white (use sterilised egg white,   *15ml (1 tbs) water*
* since this will not be cooked)*   *peeled zest of 1 lemon*
1. mix all the ingredients together in a saucepan, and heat very slowly until it simmers.
2. remove from the heat, allow to stand 5 minutes, then strain it into jelly or sherry glasses, and leave in a cool place to set

From the later nineteenth century, a savoury course was usually served after the dessert, its dishes all being small in size, but very strong in flavour, with devilled savouries, toasted cheeses etc. to promote an appetite for the liquors served at the end of the meal.

Anchovy Toast, Miss Crosland

12 anchovy fillets   *2 hard-boiled eggs*
small squares of freshly fried bread   *parsley for garnishing*
50g (2 oz) butter
1. pound the anchovies with the butter and egg yolks in a pestle and mortar, then rub it through a fine sieve
2. pipe the anchovy butter onto the fried bread, decorate it with chopped parsley and chopped egg white, and serve piping hot

At this stage, the ladies retired to take their tea or coffee in the drawing room, leaving the gentlemen to their port, brandy, and other strong liquors. In the seventeenth and eighteenth centuries most country house ladies were skilled distillers, making various alcoholic spirits, toilet and medicinal waters in their own well-equipped still-houses. By the nineteenth century, most domestic stills had fallen out of use, but a drink called shrub was still being made by combining citrus fruit, sugar and brandy to produce one of the smoothest and most delicious of drinks.

Orange Shrub (Healey)

300ml (¹/₂ pt) rum or brandy   *25g (1 oz) sugar*
50ml (3 tbs) fresh squeezed orange juice, and the peeled zest of an orange
1. use a funnel to pour the sugar, then the spirit, into a bottle, seal it, and shake it until the sugar is dissolved
2. add the orange juice and zest, shake the bottle twice a day for a week, then strain the liquid through a coffee filter paper, pour into a clean bottle, and seal. It will last indefinitely, and is drunk as a liqueur

Lemon brandy

600ml (1 pt) brandy	*4 lemons*
225g (8 oz) sugar	*350ml (13 fl. oz) milk*

1. Pare the yellow zest from 2 of the lemons and put them in a bowl with the juice of the 4 lemons, and the sugar

2. heat the milk up to boiling point and pour it scalding hot into the brandy etc., cover the bowl with a large lid or a piece of plastic film etc.

3. stir the mixture twice a day for a week, then strain it through a coffee filter paper, and bottle for use

As these recipes clearly show, country house food and drink really were of the very highest quality, setting standards which it would be very difficult to equal, let alone surpass, in most modern hotels and restaurants.

On 28th July, 1904, the Rev. A.E.Salmon (at the head of the table) married William Hayes and Margaret Harland, who sit near him, to the left. This photograph, taken inside the photographic studio, shows the table set for their reception, with all the cake stands, doileys, crewets, china ware and floral decorations proper for such an important occasion.

Punch, cups, and other alcoholic drinks were served in vessels such as this Elsinore bowl, bought by Joseph Harrison, Captain of the 'Mary Eliza', a Whitby whaler, in 1854. (456-457)

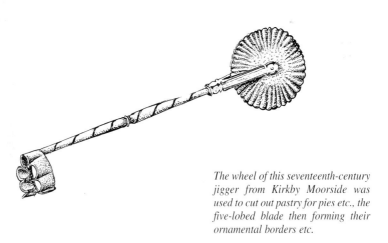

The wheel of this seventeenth-century jigger from Kirkby Moorside was used to cut out pastry for pies etc., the five-lobed blade then forming their ornamental borders etc.

Traditional Celebrations

Whether within the largest country house, or the smallest cottage, everyone looked forward to the perpetual sequence of traditional ceremonies which marked the progress of the year. Most, like Christmas and Easter, were great Christian festivals which took place on definite days, while others, such as the churn and mell suppers held at the end of harvest, could vary from one season to another, representing customs which must have originated thousands of years before the first Christian missionaries arrived in these islands.

At each of these events, a distinctive range of foods was served. These formed a major feature of the celebration, appearing only at the appropriate time of year, in contrast to today, when commercial interests put Easter eggs into the shops in early January, and Hot Cross Buns can often be found months away from Good Friday. One of the characteristics of the foods made and served at these special events was that they were all extremely old-fashioned, the menus of these celebration meals retaining dishes which had disappeared out of the everyday diet centuries ago. A good example is frumenty, a dish of unground wheat, soaked, beaten and stewed to form a glutinous whole-grain porridge. This is perhaps our oldest cooked food, representing the way in which pre-historic people made their carefully-gathered stocks of wild grass seeds much more palatable and digestible, but it is still made for Christmas Eve in some Yorkshire families today, representing one of the world's oldest continuous cooking traditions.

In a similar manner, today's communal family Christmas dinner, where the family sit down together and eat a meal comprising perhaps a soup, a large roast and a rich boiled pudding, are enjoying a good middle-class meal of about 150 years ago. In many homes this represents a considerable contrast to their normal pattern of eating, where the complexities of work, school and leisure interests can mean that they rarely eat together, and even if they do, they would never make a boiled suet pudding, since this had gone out of fashion two or three generations into the past.

Although these festive foods represent a long and continuous tradition, some of the individual dishes, and their related events, have gradually changed over the years. As dried fruit became much cheaper in the Victorian period, for example, both minced pies and Christmas puddings became almost unpleasantly rich and heavy. Similarly the old yeast-raised and lightly-fruited Yule cakes were replaced by the richly-fruited egg-raised Christmas cakes, while hard-boiled hen's eggs for Easter were replaced by chocolate or sugar Easter eggs bought from the confectioner's.

Today we celebrate fewer of our traditional events than we did a century ago, the churn and mell suppers, All Soul's, Back End and St.Thomas's Day being amongst those which have now disappeared. However, various writers, and the recipes written down by local housewives, still enable us to describe them, and to re-create their special foods.

Working through the year, following the end of Christmas on Twelfth Night, the first major events marked the onset of Lent. The day before Shrove Tuesday was called Collop Monday, when collops, slices of bacon or ham, were eaten with fried eggs, this being a survival of the medieval practice of eating the last of the preserved meats before the long fast throughout Lent. In the poorer homes the collops might have to be begged from wealthier neighbours, and the fat they produced saved to fry the pancakes on the following day.

On Shrove Tuesday, or Pancake Day, it was customary for the church bells to be rung around 11am as a signal for the housewives to start making the pancakes, perhaps using recipes such as the following, from Miss Crosland;

Mr Atkinson's Excellent Pancakes

75ml (5 tbs) flour	*225ml (8 fl.oz) milk*
pinch of salt	*225ml (8 fl.oz) water*
1 egg	*lard for frying*

1. mix the flour and salt in a bowl, make a well in the centre, break in the egg and half the milk and water, beat to a smooth batter, then beat in the remaining liquids
2. stand for 1 to 2 hours
3. fry in hot lard. Serve with lemon juice and sugar, or Golden syrup

The evening was traditionally called 'toffee boiling night' or 'join night', when people clubbed together to buy the ingredients for making a batch of toffee which they then shared out amongst themselves. On one of these occasions, Miss Crosland collected;

H.F.Jewson's Toffee. Shrove Tues. 1934

550g (1¼lb) Demarara sugar	*30ml (2 tbs) water*
100g (4 oz) butter	*15ml (1 tbs) vinegar*
150g (6 oz) Golden syrup	*15ml (1 tbs) lemon juice*

1. put all the ingredients into a saucepan, and warm them very slowly, not allowing them to boil, and stirring regularly, for 30 minutes.
2. boil the toffee quickly for a few minutes, test a piece by dropping it into cold water, then remove the pan from the heat, leave it for a few minutes, then pour it into a shallow well-buttered tin and leave to set

Fritters were eaten on Ash Wednesday, these being made of fruit, eggs and spices, bound with flour and raised with yeast. One eighteenth century Yorkshire recipe gives the following instructions[1];

Fritters

2 eggs	*2 medium eating apples, grated*
225g (8 oz) flour	*12g (½ oz) candied peel*
25g (1 oz) yeast	*pinch of ground nutmeg*
50g (2 oz) currants	*225ml (8 fl.oz) tepid milk*
50g (2 oz) caster sugar	*grated rind & juice of a lemon*

1. mix the dry ingredients, make a well in the centre, pour in the eggs, and beat these in, with the yeast dissolved in the milk, then leave the batter in a warm place for 2 to 3 hours
2. drop large spoonfulls into lard boiling in a frying pan, brown on both sides, then serve immediately, sprinkled with sugar

On the next day, known as Bloody Thursday, black puddings were eaten.
      A few weeks later, the fourth Sunday in Lent was celebrated as Carling Sunday;[2]
      'Carlin' Sunday we kep up
      Wi' grey pez cooked fer t'supper.
      They're steeped i'watter ower neet,
      Then fried wi' saim or butter'
Carlings were grey or brown dried peas which, having been soaked in water overnight, were drained, placed in a pan of boiling water with a pinch of salt and simmered about twenty minutes. Having been drained once more, they were then fried in butter or lard for two or three minutes before being served with either salt and pepper or sugar and vinegar. Along the coast from the Humber to the Tyne there are various legends of how carlings

first arrived as the cargo of a ship driven ashore by storms, the peas, soaked and swollen by the sea water, then being gathered by the famine-stricken population living along the shore. These stories appear to be apocryphal, for carlings were cooked and eaten in central Yorkshire too, many miles inland. In the 1860s two or three hundredweight of carling peas were sold each year in some of the small North Riding towns, but today the custom has virtually disappeared.

On Good Friday, it was usual for children to go round their neighourhood to beg their 'pace eggs', this name coming from 'paschal', relating to Easter. It was also the day for eating Hot Cross Buns, and for making Good Friday Cakes, for it was believed 'That if we do eat of a Cake made purposely on Good Friday we shall never want Money or Victuals all the Year Round which for many years...has always fallen out true'. Even in the 1870s, best flour biscuits were made in Whitby, holes pierced through their centres allowing them to be strung from the ceiling throughout the following year. They were believed to cure diarrhoea when grated into either milk or brandy and water whenever required.[3]

'On Heeaster Sonda' we've Peeast Eggs,
An' lots o'Kustods teea;
An' if you've nowt to put on new,
There is a fine to dea'[4]

Here, at the end of Lent, when eggs were permitted once more, it was customary to start making egg custards.

Baked Custards

2 eggs   *225g (8 oz) shortcrust pastry*
300ml ('/₂ pt) milk   *pinch of grated nutmeg*
15ml (1 tbs) sugar
1. Roll out the pastry and use it to line a 20cm (8 inch) flan tin
2. fill the case with bran or baking beans, and bake at 200°C, 400°F, gas mark 6 for 10 minutes, then remove from the oven, and remove the bran or beans
3. beat the eggs well, beat in the sugar, and then the milk, pour this into the pastry case, grate the nutmeg on top, and bake at 180C, 350F, gas mark 4 for about 30 minutes until the custard is firmly set

By Easter Monday the pace eggs would have been boiled hard and decorated, the basic staining of the eggs usually been carried out by tying either coloured rags (when their dies were not so fast as they are today) or the outer skins of onions around them and boiling them for half an hour, after which they could be polished with a little butter. Each family had their own way of decorating the eggs, perhaps using natural colourings such as cochineal, or spring flowers, or writing or painting names or messages, for it was important that each individual egg could be recognised by its owner when they were rolled down the grassy slopes of a nearby hill. Maggie Newbery could remember rolling her eggs down Brandsby Hill around 1905.[4] If they managed to reach the bottom intact, it was believed to be a sign of good luck for the coming year, but most hit stones and cracked, then being spreedily peeled and eaten on the spot. It was quite a social occasion, with the mothers sitting and talking at the top of the hill while the children chased their eggs. The lads, meanwhile, used a much speedier way of either adding to their store of food, or loosing their eggs, by 'jauping' one against another, the broken one being forfeited to the winner.

After Easter, the next events took place around early May, these being the survivors of the old pagan May-day celebrations whch had been so severely suppressed during the

Commonwealth. At Slingsby, for example, the maypole was erected on May 14th, cheesecakes and spice bread being collected from the houses to furnish a communal 'rearing tea', which was followed by dancing to the music of the local brass band.[5]

Late spring and summer were also popular times for non-conformist chapel anniversaries, when the local congregation was joined by others from neighbouring chapels for a day of praise, with hymns, prayers and readings. At Levisham Primitive Methodist Chapel, for example, 'There were special preachers on the Sunday, and on the next day the tea-feast was held in the Chapel, and lemon-cheese cakes and curd-cheese cakes, and good tea and rich cream were enjoyed by everyone. Then a public meeting was held in Mr Dixon's big barn, and recitations, speeches and hymn-singing ended the day'[6] There were Sunday School outings too, the children being taken off for the day, perhaps on horse-drawn waggons to a local beauty spot, or by railway to the coast, a picnic being packed up beforehand. One Claxton lady remembered a Sunday School visit to Millington, where the local farmer's wife boiled the water for the tea, which was made in a bucket ready for their picnic at the side of the springs where they had been paddling.[7]

The prosperity of each farmer and farm worker depended on the completion of a successful harvest each year, this being the culmination of a year-long effort to enrich the soil, sow and cultivate the crops, and bring them safely home in spite of the depredations of birds, weeds and foul weather. For these reasons, the end of harvest was always marked with a celebration party, with food, drink and other entertainments. Sometimes it was called a kern, or churn supper, with cakes and cream etc. held after the cutting of the last sheaf, but it could also be called a mell or meyl supper, held after all the crops had been led back to the farm. William Marshall of Pickering described the mell-supper as 'a supper given to farm work-people at the close of harvest, or harvest-home'.[8] Its centrepiece, the mell-sheaf, the last one cut from the harvest-field, was 'tastefully made of various kinds of corn plaited together and covered with ribbons, flowers etc. When the guests were ready for the dance, the mell sheaf would be placed in the middle of the room, which was frequently a disused one, and they danced round it. It was made like a figure, and was sometimes called the mell-doll'. This was at Kilburn early in the nineteenth century.[9]

The kinds of food served at these occasions back in the seventeenth century had included 'puddings, bacon or boyled beefe, flesh or apple pyes, and then creame brought in platters and every one a spoone; then, after all they have hot cakes and ale; for they bake cakes and send for ale against that time. Some will cut their cake and put it into their creame, and this feast is called the creame-potte, or creame-kitte'.[10] The cakes, probably a variety of turf or girdle cakes, were made rather thick and sweet with carraway seeds and currants, and were crossed on their top by small squares cut into their dough just before baking.

In the eighteenth century Eugene Aram, the infamous Knaresborough murderer, recorded that 'from time immemorial, it was customary to produce in a churn, a great quantity of cream and to circulate it by dishfulls to each of the rustic company, to be eaten with bread. And here sometimes very extraordinary execution has been done upon cream. And, though this custom has been dismissed in many places and agreeably commuted for by ale, yet it survives still and that about Whitby and Scarborough'.[11] In this area, a hundred years later, 'a large China bowl in some houses replaced the churn, and new milk, or even furmity, did duty for the cream'.[12] Within living memory, across the Moors at Ainthorpe in Eskdale, Mr F.Raw told Marie Hartley and Joan Ingiby how 'For the last sheaf, everybody was there and each tied a band round it. At night my father cut them all loose so that the corn could dry. For the last tea-time mell-cakes were brought into the field, cut in four, split, buttered, sprinkled with sugar and nutmeg. There was a milk bucket full of tea, and fun with rabbits at the end'.[13]

For the mell suppers, meat, cakes and tarts might precede the dancing, with cakes and ale for refreshment afterwards, as described in the following poem;[14]

> 'An' what Mell-suppers there was then!
> All't warkfooaks went seea smart;
> They'd tea, an' beef, an' ham, an' then
> They'd lots o'keeak an' tart
>
> An' efter t'meeat was clear'd away,
> They set out t'yall an' gin;
> An' when t'awd fiddler play'd a tune,
> Now t'lads meead t'lasses spin!...
>
> Then keeakk an' yall was handed round,
> A gud few tahms through t'neet;
> They nivver thowt o'gahin off yam
> Tell it was breead dayleet'

Later in the year, parkin had to be baked ready for Bonfire Night. Originating as soul-mass cakes, or thar-cakes, eaten on All Soul's night on November 2nd, they became associated with the anniversary of the Gunpowder Plot just three days later. The following local recipe, probably dating from the 1830s, produces a light, fine-textured cake;[15]

Parkin Gingerbread

225g (8 oz) flour
100g (4 oz) sugar
100g (4 oz) treacle
50g (2 oz) butter
150ml (1/4 pt) milk
2.5ml (1/2 tsp) bicarbonate of soda
50g (2 oz) candied peel
10ml (2 tsp) ground ginger
1. line a large loaf tin, or an 18cm (7 inch) round tin with greased greaseproof paper
2. mix the flour, sugar, bicarbonate of soda, ground ginger and candied peel in a bowl
3. place a small saucepan on the scales, note the weight, then weigh in the treacle, add the butter, and warm them together until melted
4. pour the treacle into the dry ingredients and stir, while pouring in the milk, to form a smooth mixture
5. pour the mixture into the tin, and bake at 150C, 300F, gas mark 2, for 1 1/2 hours

Most of the traditional parkin recipes include oatmeal, these versions from Jane Trenham of Sinnington's recipe book of 1881 using first fine oatmeal and a large proportion of treacle, and the second coarser oatmeal with very little treacle, to produce contrasting textures and flavours.

Parkin

225g (8 oz) fine oatmeal
2.5ml (1/2 tsp) bicarbonate of soda
10ml (2 tsp) ground ginger
225g (8 oz) treacle
25g (1 oz) butter
150ml (1/4 pt) beer
1. line a loaf tin or an 18cm (7 inch) round tin with greased greaseproof paper
2. mix the oatmeal, bicarbonate of soda and ginger together
3. place a small saucepan on the scales, weigh in the treacle, add the butter, and warm them together until melted
4. Pour the treacle into the dry ingredients, and stir in with the beer to form a stiff mixture

5. pour the mixture into the tin, and bake at 150°C,300°F, gas mark 2, for 1½ hours

Treacle Parkin

450g (1 lb) medium oatmeal
100g (4 oz) sugar
10ml (2 tsp) ground ginger
25g (1 oz) treacle

50g (2 oz) butter
50g (2 oz) lard
15ml (1 tbs) beer or water

1. line a tin as in the recipe above
2. mix together the oatmeal, sugar and ginger
3. place a small saucepan on the scales, weigh in the treacle, butter and lard, warm them together until melted, pour it into the oatmeal etc., add the water or beer, and stir to form a stiff paste
4. tip the mixture into the tin, fork it level, then bake at 150C, 300F, gas mark 2, for 1½ to 1¾ hours

As with other parkins and gingerbreads, these last two examples should be stored for a few weeks before being eaten, for only then will they 'come again', and develop their full flavour, moisture and stickyness.

The next great celebration to look forward to was Christmas, which really started on St Thomas' Day, December 21st, the shortest day of the year, when children or old people walked from one of the larger houses to another, begging for small supplies of wheat. On this day too, the corn millers gave to their customers, the retail flour-dealers, a portion of pearled wheat, which they in turn gave away to their customers. To pearl the wheat, it was put into a large sheet-iron cylinder which had been pierced with a sharp punch to give it a rough internal surface, like a coarse grater. As this cylinder rotated in one direction, a millstone with radiating grooves (507) set within it, rotated in the opposite direction, the combined effect of the iron grater and the rough stone being to grind off the outer husk, leaving just the smooth inner grain. The commercial bakers bought the pearled wheat in this form, then soaking and boiling it until it 'creed' into a soft, swolen mass, finally thickening it with flour before ladling it into basins. When cool, it solidified into a stiff jelly which could be turned out and arranged in pyramidal mountains in the shop window ready for sale.

The wheat which had been collected by Thomasing or gleaning, or which had come into the house at harvest time and being hung from the rafters at the end of the kitchen nearest the fire, had to be de-husked before it could be used. In some households this was carried out by pouring the grain into a clean stack and beating it with sticks upon the floor. A white sheet was then spread on the floor near the open door and the grain poured onto it from a plate, thus allowing the chaff to be blown away by the draught. In other houses the grain was first soaked in water before it was beaten in the sack, the chaff rising to the surface when the grain was washed in water. The cleaned grain was then placed in a pan or stoneware jar, covered with three times its own volume of water, and left in a hot oven for a day and a half until it was creed ready for Christmas eve. The way in which this dish was cooked varied from one household to another, but was usually made as follows;

Frumenty

600ml (1 pt) creed wheat
600ml (1 pt) milk
40g (1½ oz) flour

2.5ml (½ tsp) allspice, nutmeg or cinnamon
50g (2 oz) treacle

1. mix the milk into the flour, bring both to the boil, stirring continuously, then add the remaining ingredients
2. re-heat to boiling point, then pour out into basins and serving immediately. For a richer mixture, about 100g (4 oz) currants could be cooked with the frumenty. Many modern recipes which include butter, cream, sugar, rum or brandy produce something rather like a liquid Christmas pudding

The period before Christmas eve was also the time to complete all the baking which would be required over the holiday period. First to have been made would be the gingerbreads or peppercakes, for some of these had to be stored for weeks or months to soften, mellow and mature ready for Christmas. Some of the earlier recipes appear to have used yeast as their raising agent;

Pepper Cake, Mrs Hobson

450g (1 lb) treacle   *15ml (1 tbs) carraway seed*
400g (14 oz) plain flour   *15ml (1 tbs) brandy*
12g (¹/₂ oz) butter   *50g (2 oz) candied peel*
10ml (2 tsp) ground ginger   *12g (¹/₂ tsp) yeast*

1. bruise the carraway seed in a pestle and mortar, then mix it with the flour, ginger,and carraway seed, rub in the butter, and mix in the candied peel
2. dissolve the yeast in 150ml (¹/₄ pt) water at blood heat, and stir this, with the treacle, into the flour etc, to form a soft dough
3. cover the dough and leave it in a warm place for about an hour until it has doubled in size, then lightly knead it, place it in an 18cm (7 inch) round tin, and leave to rise once more, then bake at 150°C, 300°F, gas mark 2 for about 1¹/₂ hours

Later recipes use bicarbonate of soda instead of yeast, as may be seen in the following account;[16]

Gingerbread Roll baked at R.Simson's Jan 6th. About 41/2d (2p) the lb.

lb.	oz.		s.	d.	(modern metric measure)
3	8	Treacle	1	2	400g
0	4	Cinnamon	0	4	25g
1	4	Sugar	0	2	125g
0	2	Seasoning	0	2	12g (mixed spice)
1	6	Butter	1	0	135g
4	0	Flour	0	10	450g
			4	3	

4d for baking
pint of warm milk   *150ml*
small teaspoon c. Soda   *5m (bicarbonate of soda)*

1. line an 18cm (7 inch) round tin with greased greaseproof paper
2. rub the butter into the flour, stir in the sugar, spices and soda, and make a well in the centre
3. mix in the milk, and the warmed treacle, little by little to form a soft dough
4. place the dough into the tin and bake at 150°C, 300°F, gas mark 2 for 1¹/₂ hours, then store for a week or two before use

For a lighter alternative, Jane Trenham of Sinnington made an egg-raised white gingerbread;

White Gingerbread

225g (8 oz) butter	225g (8 oz) flour
225g (8 oz) sugar	100g (4 oz) candied peel
3 eggs	25g (1 oz) ground almonds
15ml (1tbs) ground ginger	

1. Line an 18cm (7 inch) round tin with greased greaseproof paper
2. cream the butter with the sugar, beat in the eggs, stir in the peel and almonds, and fold in the flour
3. bake at 150C,300F, gas mark 2 for about 1½ hours

Many families preferred to buy their gingerbreads from the bakeries which traded in virtually every small town. The Sonleys of Kirkbymoorside, for example, had made moulded gingerbreads from at least the early nineteenth century. The stiff dough was made using recipes such as;

Moulded Gingerbreads

450g (1 lb) flour	5ml (1 tsp) each of ground corriander
225g (8 oz) treacle	carraway, cinnamon & allspice
50g (2 oz) brown sugar	15ml (1 tsp) ground ginger
50g (2 oz) lard	

1. line a 12cm (5 inch) square tin with greased greaseproof paper, and tie a few layers of paper around the base and sides of the tin to provide extra insulation
2. mix the dry ingredients, rub in the lard, and stir in the warmed treacle, then kneading it to form a very short, crumbly mix
3. press the mixture hard down into the tin (the old bakers used to put a board on top and stand on it) and either smooth the top, or decorate it. Some families used to decorate the top by impressing it with overlapping prints from the rim of an egg-cup
4. bake at 130°C,250°F, gas mark 1-2 for 1 to 1½ hours. Store for a few weeks in a cold, damp room before using

To mould the gingerbread, the mixture was traditionally packed in a wooden box or frame reinforced with a sheet iron base and corners (92-93). A mould carved either in wood (89-90) or in stone (91) was then placed on top and the whole lifted down onto the floor, so that it could be firmly stamped underfood to produce a really clear print. The mould was then removed, leaving the gingerbread inside its wooden frame, which now served as an insulated baking tin while it cooked in the oven. The most popular designs featured crude versions of the Royal arms, but others bore geometric patterns, owls, or sprays of holly, mistletoe and the Christmas goose appropriate to the season.

Next came the Yule cakes, originally made with a fruited and spiced yeast dough;

Mary Sugden's Old Fashioned "Spiced loaf" for Christmas (Miss Crosland)

50g (2 oz) butter	100g (4 oz) valencia raisins
25g (1 oz) lard	100g (4 oz) currants
225g (8 oz) flour	50g (2 oz) candied peel
50g (2 oz) sugar	12g (½ oz) yeast

pinch grated nutmeg

150ml (¼ pt) milk

1 egg, beaten

1. rub the butter and lard into the flour, stir in the sugar and nutmeg, the raisins, currants and peel

2. dissolve the yeast in 80ml (3 fl. oz) water at blood heat, and mix this in with the milk, also warmed to the same temperature, mix this into the dry ingredients to form a soft dough, cover this over, and leave it in a warm place for about an hour until doubled in size

3. lightly knead the dough with a little flour, place it in a large greased loaf tin, and leave it in the warm until it has risen to fill the tin

4, bake at 150C, 350F, gas mark 4 for about 1¼ hours, covering the top with a little greaseproof paper if necessary to prevent the fruit etc from scorching

Later varieties used bicarbonate of soda instead of yeast, as seen in the following local recipe of 1873;[17]

A Light Spice Loaf

225g (8 oz) flour

100g (4 oz) currants

50g (2 oz) butter

50g (2 oz) candied lemon peel

225g (8 oz) sugar

80ml (3 fl.oz) cream

2 eggs, beaten

5ml (1tsp) bicarbonate of soda

1. line an 18cm (7 inch) round tin with greased greaseproof paper

2. rub the butter into the flour, then stir in the sugar, currants, peel, and bicarbonate of soda, then make a well in the centre and work in the eggs and cream to make a soft mixture

3. place the mixture in the tin and bake at 140C, 325F, gas mark 3 for about 1½ hours

As in other parts of the country, these spiced yule cakes were gradually superseded by richer plumb cakes or Christmas cakes during the late Victorian period. They used eggs for raising, and included more dried fruits, almonds etc since the expanding British Empire had now made these much cheaper than they had ever been before.

A Rich Plumb Cake, Jane Trenham

150g (6 oz) butter

75g (3 oz) candied peel

150g (6 oz) caster sugar

75g (3 oz) flaked almonds

4 eggs, beaten

75g (3 oz) chopped citron

15ml (1 tbs) treacle

325g (12 oz) currants

50ml (2 fl.oz) brandy

few drops almond essence

1. cream the butter with the sugar, and then beat in the eggs, treacle and brandy, and then the remaining ingredients

2. place the mixture in a tin lined with greased greaseproof paper, with a few layers of paper wrapped around the outside for extra insulation, and bake at 150°C, 300°F, gas mark 2 for 2½-3 hours

Christmas Cake, G.Yeomans

100g (4 oz) butter

50g (2 oz) glace cherries

100g (4 oz) sugar

50g (2 oz) almonds

3 eggs

50g (2 oz) mixed peel

150g (6 oz) flour

50g (2 oz) sultanas

2.5ml (½ tsp) mixed spice

50g (2 oz) valencia raisins

2.5ml (½ tsp) baking powder

50g (2 oz) currants

15ml (1 tbs) treacle   *grated rind of a lemon*
few drops vanilla essence
Follow the method given for the recipe above

The mincemeat had also to be made ready for the numerous pies required both for the family and for their visiting friends and relations. In earlier centuries mincemeat was literally that, minced mutton being the usual meat, with a little dried fruit and spices to enrich its flavour, but by the late eighteenth century, however, the meat content had virtually disappeared, only the suet remaining in a mixture which now comprised apples, dried fruits, sugar and lemons. To today's taste the traditional recipes contain far too much suet, and so the quantity has been halved in the following version;

Mincemeat (incomparable), Mrs St. A.Wood
2 lemons   *325g (11 oz) sugar*
100g (4 oz) suet   *15ml (1 tbs) brandy*
325g (11 oz) currants   *50ml (2 oz) candied peel*
1. squeeze the lemons, scrape out the fibrous pulp, then simmer the peels in a little water for some 20 minutes until tender
2. drain the peels, liquidise them, or pound them in a mortar to form a smooth paste
3. mix half the lemon juice with the peel paste and the remainder of the ingredients, then use fresh as modern mincemeat

Having made these preparations, the Christmas celebrations could begin on Christmas Eve, when everyone gathered around the living room table after dusk. First the yule log saved from last Christmas Eve was place on the fire, and from this the master or the youngest daughter in the house lit the yule candle in the middle of the table, all other lights being extinguished. Next a cross was scraped across the top of an uncut cheese, placed on a large platter or dish. The pepper cake was then placed on top of the cheese, the master then cutting them in pieces for everyone coming to the house, inviting them 'noo, ye mun taste our cheese', and usually offering them an accompanying glass of wine or spirits, after which everyone offered their good wishes for the season.[18] Only then was the frumenty served.

On Christmas Day, the first concern was to get everything ready for dinner, especially the meat. Many households roast a large joint of beef, but those who could afford it usually preferred to cook a goose, even though they were always expensive at this time of year, the price representing around a week's wages for many of the poorer people. In the 1880s George Wright always bought the family's goose for his brother John, licensee of the White Horse Inn at Beadlam, carefully noting its weight and price in his notebook;[19]

> 'December 1879 paying for a Goose Dressed...got it of Robert carpenter,
> Wombleton, weighed 9³/₄ lb at 9d (4¹/₂p) per lb, gibblets inside.
> December 26th, 1882, I paid the Misses Teasedale, Skiplam, for a Goose,
> Dressed, weighed 10 lb at 9d per lb 7s 6d (37¹/₂p)
> December 24, 1883 I paid Mrs Teasedale for a Goose weighed 11 lb at 9d per
> lb. paid 8s (40p)'

Although dressing the goose sounds quite a straightforward affair, it involved a lot of hard work. At Holly Park near Kirkby Moorside, Mrs June Wood was given the task of plucking the geese heads, poking their eyes out, and skinning their feet. The geese were then sold with everything put inside them, including all the innards, the gizard, kidneys, heart, liver, skinned feet, skinned head and crag (neck), and the ends of the wings. After the goose had been killed, it was hung up with its head over a basin of oatmeal, its throat being cut so that all the blood drained into the meal. One end of the foot-long neck skin was then tied up, stuffed with the blood and oatmeal mix, and the other end tied up to form a pudding which was also put inside to make up the weight.

When the goose arrived in the back kitchen, all the articles inside the body were taken out, chopped up, cooked, and put into a big square pie dish with a really thick crust on the top. After baking it was cut into squares, the mixture resembling stuffing, being quite delicious and, although you had to pick out all the little bones as you ate it, the bits of skin that were around the segments of oatmeal and blood were eaten as well. As for the goose itself, this was carefully roasted and served with potatoes, vegetables and all the trimmings as the main course for the Christmas dinner.

For the next course was, of course, a large Christmas pudding. The earlier puddings were much plainer than those offered for sale today, but were perhaps more suitable for the end of a large meal;

Plum Pudding, Mrs L.Hartley

225g (8oz) suet   pinch of salt
100g (4 oz) plain flour   2ml ($^1/_4$ tsp) ground ginger
150g (6 oz) currants   2ml ($^1/_4$ tsp) ground nutmeg
100g (4 oz) chopped raisins   2 eggs, beaten
a little milk

1. mix together all the dry ingredients, then stir in the eggs, and just sufficient milk to make a stiff mixture
2. pack the mixture into a pottery or metal pudding basin, filling it to the brim, place a sheet of kitchen foil over one of greaseproof paper, fold a pleat across the centre, place them over the bowl (foil uppermost), tie them down, and make a string handle across the bowl
3. place the bowl in a pan of cold water, bring it to the boil and cook for 4 hours, adding more boiling water as it evaporates or tie the pudding in a cloth to form a spherical shape, and boil it in a pot for 4 hours
4. remove the pudding from the pot, remove the foil and paper, or cloth, and serve with;

Caudle Sauce for Plum Pudding, 1873

30g (1 oz) butter   grated peel of a lemon
30g (1 oz) flour   90ml (3 tbs) sherry
600ml (1 pt) milk   30ml (2 tbs) brandy or rum
30ml (2 tbs) sugar

1. melt the butter in a saucepan, stir in the flour, and cook gently for 1 minute, stirring
2. remove the pan from the heat and gradually stir in the milk, sugar, nutmeg and lemon peel, bring to the boil slowly and continue cooking, stirring all the time, until the sauce thickens
3. After the sauce has cooked for a further 2-3 minutes stir in the sherry and spirits, and serve

After dinner there would be a suitable interval of rest to aid digestion, but before the day was past, there would be ample opportunity to sample the Christmas cake, mince pies and other delicacies which awaited in the pantry. This did not mark the end of Christmas cookery however, for in all the larger houses it was traditional to make large goose pies on St Stephen's Day, as Boxing Day was usually known. Some of these might be distributed among needy neighbours, but one was carefully stored ready for eating at Candlemas on February 2nd.[20] These pies, famed throughout the country from at least the early eighteenth century as Yorkshire Christmas Pies, were quite enormous, and contained a rich and flavoursome mass of poltry, game and tongue, as illustrated in the following recipe from the Healeys of Middleton Tyas around 1800;

'Christmas or Yorkshire Raised Pie, Mrs Wharton

The Crust
1 Peck of fine Flower, Knead it with suet, which must be well boiled. Make the whole into a very stiff paste. Bake it 6 hours
Veal forcemeat to line the Pie
2oz of lean veal, 2oz of Beef Suet, 2oz of bread crumbs, chop fine a little parsley, Lemon peel & sweet herbs & onions, pound in a Mortar, break in the Yoke and White of an egg. Mix it well together & season with pepper & salt. The Goose, Hare, Chickens, are to be boned before putting in & stuffed one into another & salted tongue as the Centre
Savoury Jelly for the top
Spread slices of lean beef & ham in a stewpan with a turnip, Carrot, Celery, 3 or 4 onions & sweet herbs. Cover it & let it stew over a slow fire till it is a good brown, then put water in & let it boil. Strain it well & make strong to Jelly. When cold take off the fat. Add salt & tarragon Vinegar to taste, clear with white of eggs & run thro' a Jelly bag.'

This magnificent pie certainly makes a most monumental finale to our tour of the traditional foods throughout the year in this region of Yorkshire.

Although there were numerous ceremonies connected with personal events such as birth, marriage and death, relatively few recipes have survived for the foods served on these occasions.[21] In some places, as soon as the baby had been born, the doctor cut a pepper cake and a cheese into just sufficient pieces for all those that were then present, further pepper cake, cheese and wine being served to all who crossed the threshold from that time up to the day of the baptism.

After weddings, meanwhile, the bridal party might be served with 'hot-pots', which were not stews, but large vessels full of hot spiced ale. On arriving at her home, she would be given a small bride cake, a little of which she would eat, and then throw the remainder over her head to ensure that they would always have enough and something to spare. After that, the groom took the plate, throwing it over his shoulder so that it would break, thus ensuring future happiness.

Brides Cake, Mrs Singles

125g (5 oz) butter	*100g (4 oz) raisins*
100g (4 oz) caster sugar	*400g (14 oz) currants*
3 large eggs, beaten	*75g (3 oz) candied peel*
125g (5 oz) flour	*50g (2 oz) flaked almonds*
2.5ml (1/2 tsp) nutmeg	*45ml (3 tbs) brandy*
1.5ml (1/4 tsp) cinnamon	*50ml (2 tbs) rosewater*

1. line an 18cm. (7 inch) round cake tin with greased greaseproof paper
2. cream the butter with the sugar, and beat in the eggs little by little
3. sift the flour with the spices, fold it into the mixture, then fold in the brandy and rosewater, and finally the dried fruit and almonds
4. bake at 150°C, 300°F, gas mark 2 for 3 hours

In this region it was customary for all those who had attended a funeral to return to the deceased's family home after the service, and there partake of a meal.[22] In the larger households stones, or even hundredweights of cooked beef, ham and bacon were placed on the table, these being followed by glasses of port wine served with crisp rounds or fingers of sponge cake called funeral biscuits. In the poorer households, where wine and biscuits proved too expensive, their place was taken by ale and spice cakes, the following recipe coming from Peggy Hutchinson's *North Country Cookery Secrets*;

Cropton Funeral Spice Loaf

225g (8 oz) flour	*50g (2 oz) sultanas*
10ml (2 tsp) baking powder	*25g (1 oz) mixed peel*
100g (4 oz) butter	*25g (1 oz) treacle, warmed*
100g (4 oz) sugar	*1 egg, beaten*
150g (6 oz) currants	*about 175ml (6fl.oz) buttermilk or skim milk*

1. line a large loaf tin with greased greaseproof paper
2. sift the baking powder with the flour
3. rub the butter into the flour and sugar, then mix in the remaining dry ingredients
4. make a well in the centre, mix in the eggs and treacle, then stirring in the milk to form a soft mixture.
5. bake at 150C, 300F, gas mark 2 for around 1½ hours

Just before Christmas, 1931, Inman Brothers of Norton bought some of the finest meat shown at the Malton Christmas Livestock Show and Sale, then displaying it to their customers. Prize Scotch or Moor wethers, hams and sides of bacon for curing hang on the shopfront, while inside are piles of four-inch thick fat bacon virtually free from any lean, moulded brawns, great ribs of beef, and numerous other succulent joints.

The larger of these mugs were used at Methodist love-feasts at Danby (left, no.467) and at Wombleton (right, no.466), while the smaller one is from Gillamoor Wesleyan Sunday School (470-72).

From at least the early nineteenth century A.E.Sonley of Kirkby Moorside made gingerbreads moulded with the Royal arms, holly and mistletoe, and various other designs. This is their delivery cart, used to carry their bakery to the local Prisoner of War camp.

Wood, Peat & Turf

By Mr B.Frank

None of the food described in the previous pages could have been cooked without good supplies of fuel gathered from the local woodland and moors. Around Hutton le Hole the children used to go out onto areas of the moors which had been burnt some four or five years before, for here the coarser heather stalks had bleached white and become loose from the ground, becoming 'cowls' which made ideal kindling for the fires, or to provide a sudden burst of heat to bring a kettle to the boil. The cowls were first gathered into bundles, or burdens, then being secured by a light cord which had a wooden toggle with two holes fitted at one end, so that the other end could be pulled tight and tied off to form a 'bodin o' cowls' ready to be carried on their backs back to the village.

In most parts of the country the word 'stick' is used to describe an insubstantial length of thin branch, but in Ryedale 'sticks' could be a foot or more in diameter, one end burning on the hearth, while the other rested half-way across the room, an effective way of managing a cooking fire, so long as it did not burn off balance, and suddenly roll into the room, scattering glowing ashes and smoke all over the place.

It was a continuous job, carrying bundles of fire sticks from the adjacent woods, only dead wood and fallen branches were taken and no damage had to be done to hedges. In one tall plantation of tall larches much frequented by 'stickers', we used a long pole with an iron hook fixed to one end to pull down the dead branches which were too high to reach otherwise (hence the expression 'By hook or by crook'). These branches, or 'grains' as we called them, were only about one and a half inches thick, and soon burned away, but they were very useful for stoking up the oven, or 'yoon', to use an old word, or to boil the set-pot for washing clothes.

For the fire on an evening someone would say 'Let's go for a shoulder stick' . This meant a small tree trunk or a branch of a tree perhaps four or five inches in diameter and several feet long. The problem was to find one just the right weight to carry. Arriving home, these had to be sawn up with the 'quart' saw, which required one person at each end to manipulate it. This saw was more widely known as a cross-cut. One of the worst features of going out for a shoulder stick was that one was liable to be too ambitious. I remember one occasion when I went on such an expedition accompanied by my younger brother. We were about two miles from home when we found two perfect shoulder sticks. They had been dead for many years, and were very dry and light in comparison to their bulk, for they were about nine inches thick. I was about eleven years old at the time. Harold was two years younger. We determined to carry these home, for normally only a man would carry logs of this size, but these were so dehydrated we realised it was just possible for us to do so, but light as they were in comparison to their size, they really were too heavy for us.

We managed to get them onto our shoulders and stagger for a hundred yards before resting, for about half the journey. Then the rests became more frequent, and finally Harold who was, of course, much smaller than I, said that he could not carry his any further. So I began to carry his and then go back for mine, until he recovered somewhat and tried again. What a triumph it was to arrive home with such fine shouldert sticks, and what satisfaction it was to know that one had accomplished a difficult task. Even when the logs were safely home there was still a problem, for they were holly trees, and we knew Father would never allow them to be burnt on the hearth in the home if he knew this, nor, for that matter, would he use a walking stick made of holly. 'It would be unlucky', he would say. Mother said that he was full of heathenish beliefs, but though Dad was easy going, he was adamant in these old customs and beliefs, so we hid the hollies, sawing and splitting them up when he was not about, contriving to burn them when he was at work.

In this area, along the southern margins of the North York Moors, peat and turf were formerly the principal fuels for the domestic hearth, but after World War 1, coal increasingly began to replace turf, though some coal had been burnt for many years before this. The first coal was brought from Newcastle upon Tyne in panniers on the backs of donkeys, which profoundly affected the lives of a people who had lived their lives largely isolated from the more sophisticated parts of England. Turf cutting practically ceased after 1940, though many people were cutting it immediately before this date.

Small quantities of peat continued to be cut, however. The last man in Hutton le Hole to do so was Norman Wall of Lund Farm. In 1943 he dug his peat from a bog known as Jewe Marr on the Rosedale moor towards Blakey Ridge. The bog was of good depth, and he worked a face of about 18.3 metres (20 yards) long by 1.5 metres (5 ft) high. Peat continued to be cut by Farndale people later than this. In 1964 Alfred Brown of Horne End, West Gill, Farndale, cut some on Blowth Moor, on the ridge between Farndale and Bransdale. Robert Foord still cut his yearly supply at Lealholme in 1970.

In the early 1920s a considerable amount of turf was cut. After cutting, women went to the moors to set up the turves to dry, by setting one turf on its edge and propping another against it. After a few weeks it was 'rooked', that is, set up into heaps rather like haycocks about 1.25 metres (4 ft) high. Mrs Teasdale of Harland Moor was still doing this in the late 1930s, and a decade earlier it was a general practice for the women of Farndale to help their menfolk in this way.

The first operation in connection with turfing was to 'bon a swizzen', that is, to burn an area of ground to get the long heather stalks out of the way. This was done in March after the moor had dried following the winter's rain and snow, but before the birds started to nest. It was a skilled operation. The wind had to be blowing towards a wet bog, a roadway, or some ground that had been burned the year before, and several men controlled the fire with long sticks. If it got out of hand it could burn hundreds of acres, and with a high wind it could travel for miles as fast as a horse could gallop.

Turf was cut in May and led home in late June or early July. It was usual to try to get it in before the hay harvest, which would begin in late July. Some of the turf was led with horse and cart or wagon, but a large proportion of it was led by sledge (494). In the dales of the high moors, Farndale, Westerdale, Danbydale, Rosedale, Glaisdale and others, the sledge was the most convenient mode of transport. The turf was cut on the ridges and hauled down deep hollow ways or gills called turf banks by local people. These led from the open moor directly into the farm yards, without crossing metalled roads. All the sledges were of a similar construction and size, though there were slight differences. Shelvings could be fitted on top if a slightly bigger load was to be carried, similar to shelvings on carts and wagons. In general, the sledges were constructed by the people who used them.

It was usual to make the turf stack near the back door of the farm-house, skilfully built like a haystack, about 2.7 by 3.6 metres (3 yards by 4). As the turves were about 60cm (2 ft) long they were rather difficult to get out. A turf rake was used, so that they could be hauled from the end of the stack without disturbing the top layer, which was designed to keep the rain out. The Ryedale Folk Museum has examples of rakes, all from Farndale (492-493). Sometimes the turf was not stacked, but put in a turf house, a shed near the back door. Lund Farm at Hutton le Hole had one of these, last used in 1943.

The turf spades (479-482) were worked by thrusting forward using the thighs. Since considerable force could be exerted, the thighs were protected by a turf knapper which occurred as a pair (487) or as a single unit to cover both thighs (483-486). The turf spade shafts and the knappers were made by the people who used them and no two were alike, although the general principles do not vary.

In some of the turf spades the required angle between blade and shaft was obtained by bending the junction between socket and blade. This was one of the weak points of the tool, and turf spades often had to be repaired and strengthened by rivetting a plate on to the implements at this position. Turf spade blades must originally have been made by blacksmiths. According to F.W.Dawson, *Goathland in History and Folklore* (1947), they werte made from shear steel. He also mentions that in Goathland two kinds of turf spade were used, a 'cock spade' and a 'hen spade', the latter having a blade shaped like a wide 'U'. The cock spade is the traditional turf spade described above. The hen spade, or 'sod spade', was used to cut very thin turf, perhaps where the ground was too shallow to use an ordinary turf spade. They were not used to cut turf for fuel, however, but to cut sods in areas of rough grass and heather, for covering potatoes in pits and other root crops that were clamped.

In the 1920s the spade blades were brought from ironmongers in the local market towns; they were made in major industrial centres like Sheffield and Birmingham. In the early part of this century George Russell of Kirkby Moorside made some, and John Wood of Bilsdale, who was more famos for the ploughs made at his foundry, also made a few.

In Glaisdale, as a prelude to peat cutting, the upper turf was removed with the turf spade and the ordinary spade. In this area very little overburden of turf needed to be removed. To remove the peat, a vertical back cut was made, and then the peat spade, with its square or rectangular blade (488-491) was thrust in horizontally from the breast of the bank. When the cutter took off a peat he laid it behind him on a barrow adapted to the job. When the barrow was full, an assistant, often the cutter's wife or daughter, wheeled the barrow about 18 metres (20 yards) and laid the peat out in 'rickles' using a four-pronged fork. This is now usually an ordinary byre fork, but formerly forks were specially made for this purpose. When dry, the peats measured approximately 41 by 10 by 6 cm (16 by 4 by 2$\frac{1}{2}$ inches).

The rickles contained twelve to fourteen peats. The bottom pair were laid parallel to each other, east and west. The next pair overlay them, north and south, and so on until the rickle was complete with six or seven pairs. The rickles might lie in orderly rows, or at random. In Farndale, a few miles from Glaisdale, a different method was used. Alfred Brown of Horne End Farm, Farndale, described how it was done. The peats were laid on the ground in the shape of a pentagon. The peats for the second pentagon were laid across the angles of the first, and so on until there were about five pentagons, one on top of the other, containing twenty five peats, but, whichever method was used, it ensured that the peats were thoroughly dried out and ready for burning before they were carted down to the house, where they would play their essential role in cooking the family's meals, and keeping them warm even on the coldest days.

The Ryedale Kitchen Catalogue

Among the numerous items housed in the Ryedale Folk Museum, there are some five hundred which are associated with the preparation and service of food and drink. Virtually all of them were collected from Ryedale, most from within about a ten mile radius of Hutton le Hole, since it was the policy of both Mr Crosland and Mr Frank to collect only Ryedale material. However, only for a fairly limited number of examples is there a complete record of where the individual artefacts came from.

One of the really interesting aspects of this collection is that it clearly illustrates many of the unique features of this area, those which give it its particularly distinctive character. These include the turf-burning fireplaces and the cowl-rakes used to manage them, the built-in salt-boxes, and the regional patterns of chimney cranes and reckon hooks, ginger bread moulds etc. There are also examples of the completely unglazed red earthenware kitchen pottery which was made and used locally well into the nineteenth century (55,56 & 321). In addition, there are examples of the various kitchen wares which were brought into the area from the major manufacturing centres following the arrival of the railways in the Victorian period, such as the cast iron kettles and pans from the Black Country, or the stoneware jars from Derbyshire. Most importantly, however, this collection shows how skilled craft workers, foundrymen, blacksmiths, coppersmiths, woodworkers and potters all made their wares to be thoroughly well-designed and soundly constructed to meet the needs of people who required them to prepare the food which was essential for maintaining the health and comfort of their families.

Here these artefacts are all described according to their function, as set out in the Social History and Industrial Classification, slightly modified to suit the particular needs of this collection. Details of their materials and construction are given, their dimensions in millimetres, any distinguishing marks, the name of the donor, if known, and the museum accession number, which is preceded by an A,B,C or E.

Storage

1. Salt box, stone, top stone c.20x650x405, bottom stone c.415x685x370. From a thatched cottage in Low Farndale
2. do., top stone 210x803, bottom stone 360x805,with oak spice cupboard 305x302 above. From Stang End, Danby.
3. Salt box, pine, nailed construction, grained, 409x154x321 A1680
4. Flour tub, pine with ash bands, 247x265d A1003
5. do. with ash and hardwood bands, lid missing, 238x260d C6235
6. do. painted buff with light brown bands, 248x253d 1997.13.1 Miss Evans, Scarborough
7. do. pine with beech? bands, wire bow handle with turned wooden grip, 160x165d lid missing
8. Jar, brown salt-glazed stoneware, barrel-shaped body with incised bands, 158x93d
9. do. internal white slip, rouletted border one-third down the body, 212x122d C6049
10. do. 202x108d. C5258
11. do. 148x85d C9938
12. do. white slipped interior, 317x180d C5475
13. do. stamped '1' in circle on base, 105x76d 81/35
14. do. single groove around rim, cylindrical body, 112x109d C5152
15. do. with verical grooves down body, 134x93d 1992.21.27
16. do. grey stoneware with iron dip down to just beneath a plain moulded shoulder, 204x144d. C6050
17. do. with beaded moulding at shoulder, 197x149d. C9818
18. do. stamped 'BAILEY & CO/ FULHAM' just above base, 195x148d C9622
19. Food/Livery cupboard, oak, joined construction with panelled back, oak drawer linings, nail construction, with grooved sides to run on bearers, and planked top and base. The corner posts

originally continued downwards to form long legs, but have been sawn off to their current height. 1445x1589x542 C6180

20. Hanging food cupboard, oak, joined construction for mid/late 17th cent. balusters and their frame, the remainder, including the planked top, being late 19th cent 635x903x823 C6164. When collected, it was reputed to have been used as a fox-box, to retain the animal until released for the hunt, but there is no evidence for this, and none of the gnawing of the balusters which would have resulted from the incarceration of only a single fox for a brief period.

21. Bread pot, buff earthenware with pulled and applied handles and internal iron-stained lead glaze. Lid missing 538x325d A929

22. do. light brown internal lead glaze 435x215d. Unglazed lid 275d A912

Preparation
Breaking
23. Sugar cutters, steel, 244x80 C6333
24. Nutcracker, turned sycamore, 25x50d C5948
25. do. iron, 123x25 C8356
26. do. 131x56 C8011
27. do. 107x27 C5508

Chopping/Mincing
28. Cleaver, iron/steel blade with wood handle, 289x85
29. Mincing knife, steel blade rivetted to cast brass shaft, rivetted through a diamond-shaped brass plate set into the turned mahogany handle, 165x156 1996/7/1 Mrs Connie Frank, Hutton-le-Hole.
30. do. steel, beech handle with brass bolts, 198x178 C6338.
31. do. rectangular blade with ogee-shaped hand-hole, and turned beech handle, 133x155 C10724
32. do. long curved steel blade, with turned wood handle fixed above each end, to be used with rocking motion, 181x440 C10762
33. Mincing knife and bowl, the knife steel, stamped 'VAUGHANS/BXXB/CAST STEEL', with beech handle secured by brass bolts, 149d. The turned sycamore bowl 90x262d. 1995/12/2 Mrs M.Brownlett, Kirkby Moorside.
34. Mincer/sausage machine, cast iron, with two spiral blades feeding a single nozzle, the body cast 'S&B RANSOM/SOLE/WHOLESALE AGENTS' and 'BURGESS & KEY/ LONDON' also oval brass plaque embossed 'HALES PATENT/SMALL SIZE/ BURGESS & KEY LICENSEES/1589' and the Royal arms, all screwed to a sycamore plank base. 147x220x130 C10543
35. Grater, tinplate, stamped and folded onto iron wire, 225x100x3 E398
36. do, 247x110x32 E398

Grinding/Pounding
37. Mortar, elm, one side missing. There is no documentation to suggest either domestic or industrial use.
38. Potato masher, turned pine, 288x72d C6631
39. do. sycamore, 304x72d 82/19/1
40. do. 280x69d A171
41. do. 203x62d C7434
42. do. 248x75, has been used as a mallet, 80/1
43. do. 248x58, also used as a mallet, A170
44. do. 269x69 C6126
45. do. ash, 209x 70
46. do. sycamore, made in two pieces, 294x79d C5903
47. do. 306x79d C6632
48. do. 372x95d C5942
49. do. 197x61d A169
50. elm, 249x75d C6162
51. beech, 301x79d C6127
52. square beech head with oak? handle fixed with a dowel, 265x68x57 C6344

Pressing

53. Lemon squeezer, fruitwood, white glazed pottery pierced bowl and plunger dowelled in place. Brass hinge. 48x243x80 C5919

54. Tongue/meat press, tinplate, seamed and soldered, with forged and cast iron and brass fittings, stamped '3' on base. 238x160d 1982/19/3 Mrs Julian, Driffield.

Mixing

55. Pancheon, pink-buff earthenware, unglazed, 215x467d at rim C11294

56. do. light red earthenware, internal white slip wiped to leave a red band at the rim, internal lead glaze. 218x490d at rim A1573

57, red earthenware, otherwise as no.56. 171x354d at rim A1572

58. red earthenware with internal white slip covered with yellow lead glaze. 177x391d at rim C5527

59. grey stoneware with internal glaze, 250x 504d at rim A1574

60. Spoon, beech, 303x59 C5349

61. do. 312x66 C6379

62. do. 203x50 C6339

63. do. 352x70 C7437

64. do. 295x52 C6148

65. do. 156x38 C5943 (alternatively for eating, or a toy?)

66. Ladle, sycamore, turned, with integral carved handle, 444x160d Probably for batter when making soft oatcakes. C6146

67. Spoon, iron, 343x59 C9769a

68. do. 397x59 C9769b

69. Balloon whisk, tinned iron wire, 259x75d C6334

70. Beater, tinned iron wire, 349x60d C6335

Straining

71. Collander, brown salt glazed stoneware, with external rouletted bands. 116x270d at rim A1575

72. do. grey interior, 104x203d at rim 1997.9.1 Mrs A.Hatton, Liverton

73. do. grey saltglazed stoneware, 144x 304d at rim 82/35/1 Miss Roberts, Pickering

74. do. buff earthenware, white slipped interior, fluted moulded exterior, all glazed, 112x62d C5994

Moulding & Shaping

Jelly moulds

75. white earthenware with cream-coloured lead glaze, octagonal with wicker basket of fruit design. Three moulded & applied feet on base 68x149x118 C5145

76. white earthenware, clear glaze, rosette and three tiers of flutes inside, base impressed 'IRON STONE CHINA/ (Staffordshire knot)/ G.BOWERS/ STAFFORDSHIRE/ POTTERIES' 155x238d at rim. This company operated the Brownhills Works, Tunstall, Staffs. between 1842 and 1868. C7190

77. white earthenware with clear glaze, a central quatrefoil design surrounded by ten tall gothic arches. Impressed 'MIDDLESBRO' POTTERY/(foul anchor)' 127x272x225 C5587.This mark was used at the Middlesbrough Pottery 1834-44, and probably by the Middlesbrough Earthenware Company up to 1852.

78. do. 120x253x199 C5588

79. do. 118x187x143 C5800

80. do. oval border mould with fluted sides and 12 knobs on top, stamped 'COPELAND','6' 62x123x161 C5146 The Spode Works, Stoke on Trent was founded in 1847, and still continues today.

81. do. octagonal rosette on top of two tiers of domed flutes. The exterior transfer-printed in black 'CORNFLOUR BLANC-MANGE/ BROWN & POLSON'S....' 112x168x117 C5584 These were sold for a shilling (5p) in 1916, rising to half a crown (12.5p) in the 1920s, and were featured in Brown & Polson's cookery books of this period.

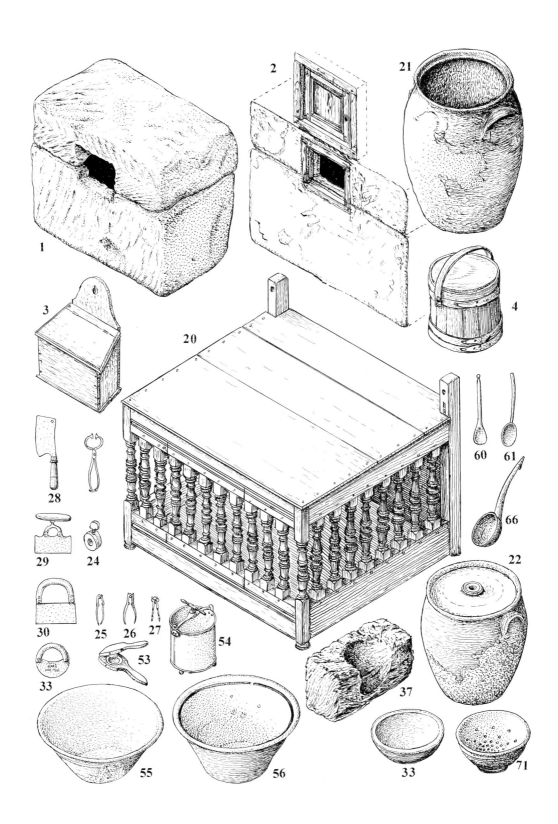

1

2

21

3

20

4

28

29   24

30   25   26   27

33

53

54

55   56

37

22

33   71

60   61

66

82. do. a spray of three gooseberries and leaves, domed fluted sides, 126x189x165 C9676

83. grey stoneware, glazed, hexagon & leaves design with domed fluted sides 105x170x137 C5585

84. brown saltglazed stoneware, a spray of three roses and leaves, fluted sides, 100x178x152 C9677

85. Little chicken moulds, tinned copper, pressed, stamped 'JONES BROS./40 DOWN ST.W,' 24x70x58 C7681 a-g These were most popular for entrees, being promoted by Mrs Agnes B.Marshall in her cookery books from the 1890s through to around the First World War.

86. do. stamped 'HARRODS STORES/LIMITED' c7681

87. Dariole moulds, tinplate, folded, seamed and wire edged 58x59d at rim B4181 a-l

88. do. fluted, 49x 55d at rim A240

Gingerbread moulds and mould/baking boxes

Numbers 89 to 95 were all used at the Sonley family's bakery in Kirkby Moorside.

89. carved fruitwood, with crowned rosette supported by a lion and a unicorn, 'H.SONLEY' above and 'G (crown)R' below. On the reverse, a similar design, but with 'KIRBY' below.

90. do. fruitwood on a pine back-board, with a crowned lion crest between 'VR IV' at the top, and 'DIEU ET MON DROIT' and the upper part of 'KIRBY' below 34x177x133 A113

91. do. sandstone, with a quatrefoil design on the front, and a wire handle set into an oval recess on the reverse A116/1

92. Mouldbox/baking box for no.91, pine, nailed construction, with sheet iron base and corner plates 111x345x268 A116/2

93. do. oak, dovetailed corners, nailed tinplate base 128x365x285 C7679

94. Cast, cement, from an 1891 Christmas gingerbread mould, showing a goose and sprays of holly and ivy 263x164x20 A115

95. do. owl and oakleaf design 150x150 x20 C5266

96. Baking board sycamore, 19x600x457 A1576

97. Rolling pin, turned ash 405x50d C5524

98. do. beech? 443x83d C6732

99. do. ash 205x28d A1824

100. do. hardwood 294x37d C5961

101. Pastry jigger, wrought iron, appears to be of 17th century workmanship 150x27x36d 1997.42.1 Mrs Maw, Kirkby Moorside.

102. Cutter, tinplate, folded & soldered, with bow handle 73x75d E 398

103. do. fluted, folded & riveted 64x65d E397

104. do, folded seam, spot welded, duck 25x80x50 C9557

105. do. bear, 25x68x42 C9557

106. do. rabbit, 25x75x43 at base C9558

107. Docker, sycamore, turned, with iron spikes 107x71d C 5267

108. do ash?, with tinplate base 106x87 C5411

109. do. tinplate, stamped, seamed & soldered 60x77d C 10302

110. Biscuit forcer, tinplate, folded & soldered, with star plate, & beech? plunger 228x41 C7044

111. Spittle, oak, 409x264x16 C5951

112. do. sycamore, 406x224x10 A1495

113. do. oak, 407x260x15 C5739

114. Riddleboard, oak, 498x457 A947

Measuring

115. Scales, balance, cast iron base, bottom of weight pan cast 'RC'. Base 150x312x117 Pressed steel ingredients pan, enamelled white above, blue below, 230d 1991.2.2 Mrs Harrison, Cropton.

116. Weights, cast iron, moulded 'C.H.CRANE WOLVERHAMPTON 4oz' 15x43d.
do. '8oz' 18x55d. do. '1lb' 18x75d. C5162

Cooking

117. Backston, cast iron plate, wrought bow with hanging hook c.290x347d A185

118. do., with raised border and fixed bow 272x335 C7204

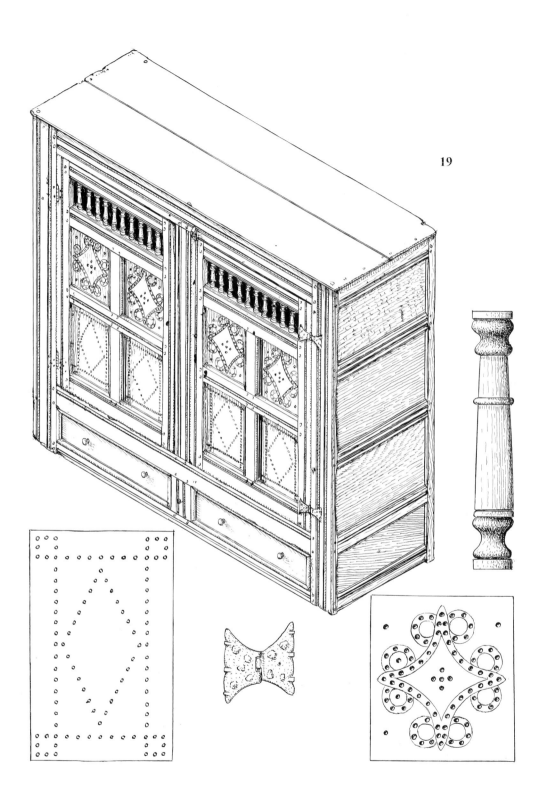

19

119. do. flat plate, folding bow with hanging ring 230x306d A180

120. do. 230x303d C5167

121. do. no hanging loop 135x228d C7176

122. Yetling, cast iron shallow pan with fixed wrought bow with hanging ring 410x430d A187

123. do. pan 372x304d. Sheet iron loop, riveted, 95x304d. Cast iron lid 318d. All A922

124. cast iron lid only 105x375d A182 Mr Walter Coverdale of Castleton, Oct 10th, 1983

125. do. 85x370d provenance as no.124

126. do. 80x345d provenance as no. 124

127. Boiling ring, cast iron, three removable boiling rings set into top 247x364d. A194 L.E.Grice, Hutton le Hole

128. Turfplate range, cast iron, turfplate moulded '...CARTER/ KIRBY', cast L-shaped boiler, sheet iron oven with facing cast 'WRELTON WORKS', damper, soot scraper, and regulators to firebox and ashpit. Stone surround with wooden mantleshelf 1594x1965 In White Cottage kitchen

129. Turfplate, moulded 'H.CARTER/KIRBYMOORSIDE' 178x1011x716

130. do. 'H.CARTER/KIRBY' 152x800x517

131. Turfplate pattern, pine, 53x992x714 This, and nos 132-4, were made by Thomlinsons of Appleton le Moor for the Carter foundry at Kirkby Moorside.

132. do. grate pattern, pine, 25x503x453 C1748

133. do. 32x403x267 C9416

134. do. 60x410x375 A1783

135. Coalgrate range, cast iron, moulded 'H CARTER/KIRBY', wrought iron crane, stone fire surround with wooden mantleshelf 1470x1622. In potting shed.

136. do. moulded 'JOSEPH CARTER KIRBY',and with a soot-scraper to the sheet-iron oven, stone surround 1720x1642. In White Cottage parlour.

137. Oven door & facing, cast iron, with added plate 'RALPH YATES/ MALTON' 957x717

138. Oven door moulded 'WALKER & CO' 435x356x10 A1763 From the Carter foundry, Kirkby Moorside.

139. Firebox/ashpit door pattern, pine, screwed, nailed, and painted dark red 192x298x36 A1751 provenance as no.138

140. Chimney crane, wrought iron, hung from the left 878x845x38 A197

141. do. hung from the right 784x842x32 C5039

142. do. 670x618x24 A196

143. do. 680x574x36 A198

144. do. 613x682x39 A199

145. do. hung from the left 655x694x37 A200

146. do. hung from the left 496x675x32 A204

147. Reckon hook, wrought iron, 7 round holes 348x46 A207

148. do. 11 holes, shortened, 353x43 A223

149. do. 8 holes 308x40 A208

150. do. 5 holes 264x45 A209

151. do. 5 holes 217x38 A212

152. do. 3 holes 185x38 A211

153. do. 6 holes, shortened, 163x34 A213

154. do. swivel hook, 9 holes 490x52 A219

155. do. 4 holes 220x 37 C5709

156. do. two hooks, nine holes 400x45 A224

157. do. cranked rack, 6 holes 242x31 C7175

158. do. keyhole-shaped holes, 6 holes 350x44 A225

159. do. 13 holes 422x46

160. do. with half-round shaft to hook, 5 holes 248x31 C5033

161. do. brass, 3 holes 56x27 C5023

162. do. with swivel hook, 10 holes 510x40 A1014

163. do. 7 holes 375x52 A221

164. Plain hook, single 110x43 A215

165. do. double hook 119x24 A217

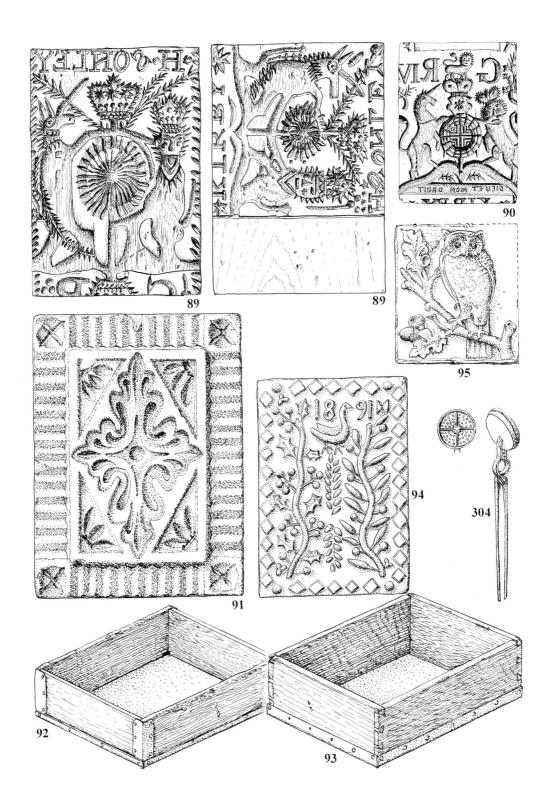

89

89

90

95

91

94

304

92

93

166. do. triple hook 196x27 C7174
167. do. 224x26 C7173
168. do. swivel 136x44x65 A211
169. do. 135x25x75 A216
170. Pot hook/ pot lifter, wrought iron, 338x41x66 A215
171. do. 255x40x71 C5712
172. do. with back strap, 288x62 C9930
173. do. 367x18x60 C9935
174. Kettle tilter, wrought iron, 173x290x60 C5028
175. Cowl-rake, wrought iron, 661x45 C6424
176. do. 365x50 A687
177. do. 364x47 C5047
178. Brig, wrought iron, fire welded 57x478x186 C10227
179. Sad-iron heater, wrought iron, riveted, 142x380x310 A710
180. Draw-plate, wrought iron, 120x380x256 A708
181. do. 145x337x198 C10226
182. do. 137x320x203 C10212
183. do. 125x 334x198 C10223
184. Firebar hook, wrought iron, fire welded & riveted, 120x310x257 C7181
185. Hearth/stove stand, wrought iron, forged & welded, with four-bar rectangular grid sliding vertically on a rod rising from a Y-shaped base 324x260x178 A928
186. Toasting fork, wrought iron on planed round hardwood handle 447x61x32d C6733
187. do. wrought iron on turned mahogany handle with brass ferule 424x110x26d
188. do. wrought iron 505x147x25 A926
189. do. steel fork on 3-part brass telescopic handle with external black enamel 299(min)x35
190. Firebar toaster, wrought iron 262x248x180 A699
191 Toasting dog, wrought iron on elm 370x472x223 1990/19/1 Used by Richard Atkinson at Kirkby Malzeard and Ripon
192. Roasting screen, pine, with ash cornice, iron fittings and tinplate lining 1660x1703x437 C6165. K.F.Hutchinson, whose family bought it in the 1920s from Stonegrave Rectory
193. Dutch oven, sheet iron, folded, wire edged and riveted, sliding on iron firebar hooks 257x387x308
194. do. 215x16x 247 C10276
195. Bottle jack, brass cased, stamped on base '30/SALTER & C0/WARRANTED' 380x106oct. A177
196. do. stamped '30/(Staffordshire knot)/WARRANTED' and on the keyhole cover plare 'Geo SALTER/IMPROVED/WARRANTED' 380x106oct. A178a
197. do. but stamped '70/SALTER & Co/WARRANTED' on base 425x126oct.
198. Bottle jack balance wheel, cast iron & iron wire 135x247d A178b
199. do. 90x170d A178c
200. Grid iron, wrought iron 656x148 C10214
201. do. riveted 85x401x199 A923
202. do. hanging 188x255x254 C10213
203. do. cast iron, white enamel lining to bars and bowl, the turned wooden handle being secured by the end of the tang being riveted over a washer 611x192 C5823
204. Frying pan, hanging, cast iron with three stub feet, riveted wrought iron bow 260x260 A188
205. do. folded sheet iron iron and an iron wire handle 63x922x413d
206. Skillet, cast bronze, moulded 'THO RUMENS' on the handle. This maker has still to be identified, see D. Eveleigh 'Cooking Pots and Old Curios-the Posnet and Skillet' *Folklife* XXXII (Leeds 1994)15. 217to rimx485x241d C5154
207. Cauldron, cast iron, wrought iron bow handle 275x356d at rim C5226
208. do. 159x235d at rim 1977.28.5
209. do. 222x292
210. do. moulded 'CARRON' on the side 358x 418d at rim
211. do. 229x350d at rim

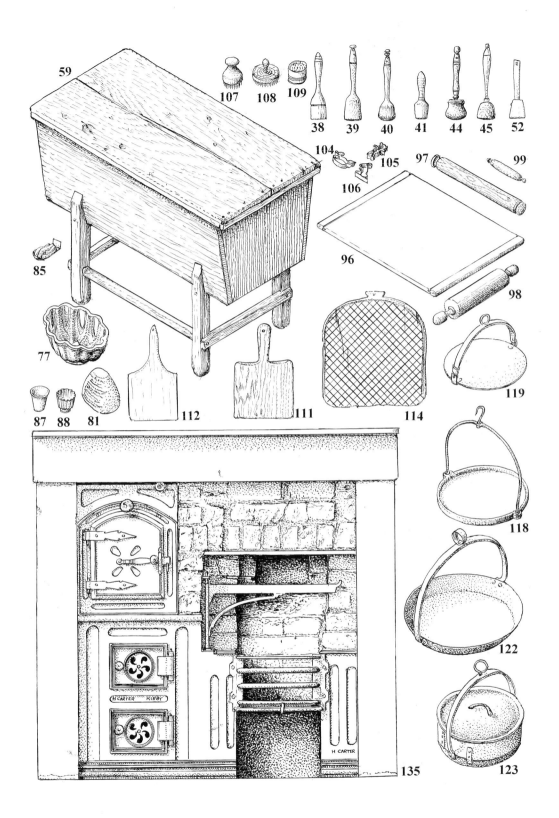

59

107 108 109

38 39 40 41 44 45 52

104
105
106

97 99

96

98

85

77

87 88 81 112 111 114 119

H CARTER KIRBY

H CARTER

135

118

122

123

212. do. cast iron, smooth hemispherical body, 3 legs, wrought iron bow hooked through semicircular projections rising above the rim   190x358d at rim A182 From Walter Coverdale of Castleton, 1983, being in his family as long as anyone could remember.

213. do. cast iron, fixed bow handle riveted to rim 510x373d C7203

214. Cauldron lid, sheet iron with riveted iron rod handle c.70x351d A184

215. Boiling pot, iron, enamelled black with grey interior, wrought iron bow handle, black enamelled brass plate on handle embossed 'JUDGE WARE' 157x213d at rim C5165

216. Stewpan, copper, dovetailed seams, rebottomed, internally tinned, wrought iron start handle with brass rivets. Matching recessed lid. Stamped 'R.BOLLANS.YORK' 122x464x29d C5173

217. Stewpan, cast iron, tubular sheet iron handle, moulded on base 'A.KENRICK & SONS/2 Pint/PATENT/No 3½' 130x133d A190

218. do. 'E.PUGH & Co/No 5 4 Pts/WEDNESBURY' 188x157d C10450

219. do. 'E.PUGH & Co/No 9 6Qts/ WEDNESBURY' 164x477x222d C10529

220. do. 'No5/ J & J SIDDONS/ WESTBROMWICH/ 4 PINTS' 112x168d C10451

221. do. 'No7/ J & J SIDDONS/WESTBROMWICH/ 4 QUARTS' 150x488x196d C10528

222. do. 'T.HOLCROFT & SONS/H/REG.MARK/ No 10/ 7 QUARTS' 179x234d C10452

223. do. unmarked 195x528x248d C10530

224. Dixie boiling pot, cast iron, oval body, wrought iron bow handle, stamped tinplate lid, its handle embossed '3' 196 to rim x385x249 C10774

225. Digester, cast iron, with tinned interior, base cast 'E.KENRICK & SONS/ 3 GALLS', wrought iron bow handle   248 to rim x248d 1990.20.1 Used by Alan Stables of Malton, Scout leader, at Scout camps before 1914

226. Preserve pan, cast brass, turned, with fixed riveted wrought iron bow stamped '1864 R.HALL' 390x324d C5138

227. do. 198x167d at rim C5544

228. do. 190x173d at rim C5566

229. do. 290x299d at rim C5567

230. do. 365x306 at rim C5569

231. do. but with handle swinging on loops riveted to the rim 142x229d C5568

232. Steamer, tinplate, folded and wire edged, with folded and riveted handles, pressed lid 540x232d 80/14 W.Goodall, Kirkby Moorside

233. do. 177x200d C9551

234. do. 354x185d A936

235. Meat fork, wrought iron 635x89 C9766

236. do. 601x94

237. do. 464x59

238. do. 439x140d C5531

239. Drainer, iron wire 439x140d C5531

240. Slice/drainer, tinned iron blade & shaft riveted onto wooden handle 425x115w C6333

241. Ladle, stamped sheet iron, rolled edge, riveted to stamped iron handle 400x115d A1023

242. Ladle or dipper, tinplate, folded, seamed & soldered, with tubular handle riveted on body 286x88d A1007

243. Stew pot, brown saltglazed stoneware, internal cream slip, 2 wad-boxed applied handles. Lid does not match 139x112

244. do. with rouletted decorative bands, lid missing 137x94d 1990.27.5 Mrs Harrison, Cropton

245. do. grey saltglazed stoneware 284x154d C6032

246. do. red earthenware, lead glazed interior and upper part of exterior, lid missing 171x165d C7976

247. Bread tin, sheet iron, folded, soldered & wire edged 95x230x164 C6025

248. do. oval, folded & wire edged, four riveted feet 77x189x136 A97

249. Bread pan, grey stoneware, glazed within, applied semicircular feet and handles 71x186x71 C5071

250. Bread tin, milk loaf, double, pressed tinplate riveted onto hinged iron bar frame 111x266x258 A136

251. Cake tin, round, folded, seamed, soldered & wire edged, with 3 scroll feet riveted on base 125x241d B4180

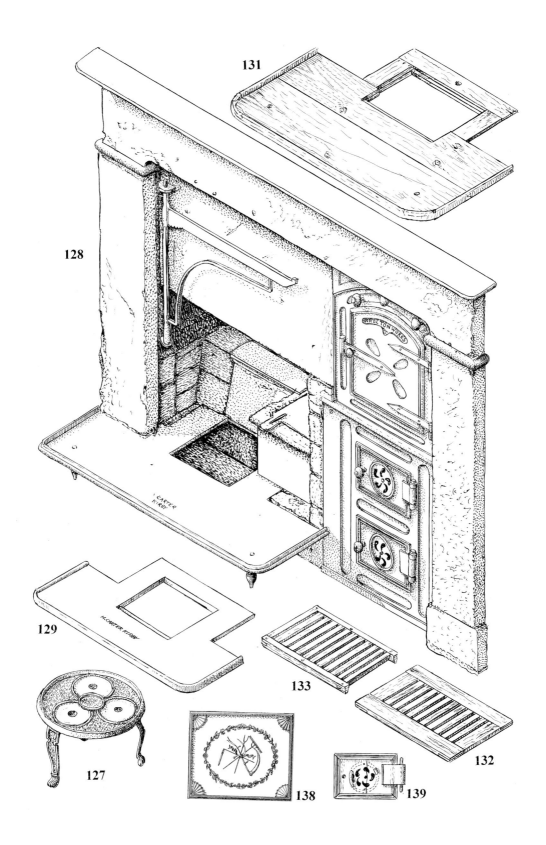

131

128

129

127

133

132

138

139

252. do. 118x208d B4179
253. do. no feet 75x156 A1591
254. Sponge cake tin, pressed tinplate, folded, seamed & soldered 121x139x122 A134
255 Tipsy cake/Savoy sponge cake tin, 3 tiers of flutes and a septagonal dome 205x 150d A135
256. do. 2 tiers of pressed tinplate flutes with pentagonal tinned copper dome, folded & seamed 233x170d A133
257. Shell tin, pressed tinplate 24x149x127 A299
258. do. A1589
259. Pie plates, pressed tinplate 35x260d 82/55/20 a-l These and nos 259-262 were collected from the workshop of R.D.Chapman, Tinsmith, of Selby.
260. do. 35x226d 82/55/19 a-d
261. do. 25x200d 82/55/18 a-c
262. do. 25x185d 82/55/17 a-c
263. Patty tins, pressed tinplate, 12x78d A124-6
264. do. 20x89d A101
265. do. 24x82d E398d
266. do. fluted, 11x81 A122-3
267. Bun tin, flat, 23x65 E398
268. do. domed, 23x62d E398
269. Queen cake tins, pressed tinplate, heart, 16x72x69 A238
270. do. diamond, 16x95x66 A128
271. do. folded & seamed, round on hexagon base 30x60 C6680
272. do. square, 20x47x47 A129
273. do. 37x59x52 1997.28.10
274. do. 38x48x63 1997.28.10
275. do. triangle 25x60 sides C6679 & C6684
276. do. diamond, 24x83x66 C6676,6683, 6687 & 6694
277. do. 21x50x79 A237 & C6675
278. do. 38x84x63 1997.28.12
279. do. 37x86x66 1997.28.12
280. do. kite shaped 21x77x55 C6677
281. do. oval 38x79x52 1997.28.15
282. do. 38x79x53 1997.28.15
283. do. heart, 39x67x65 1997.28.11
284. do. 36x65x69
285. do. 39x65x67
286. do. pentagonal 26x40-43 sides C6693
287. do. hexagonal 25x68d C6678
288. do. elongated octagon 23x77x53 C66898
289. do. 21x72x51 A130
290. do. 27x74x49 C6682
291. do. club 22xc.60d C6686
292. do. 23x67x59 C6690
293. do. 33x70x66 1997.28.14
294. do. quatrefoil 40x58x55 1997.28.13
295. do. crescent 22x65d C6692
296. do. 37x68x58 1997.28.7
297. do. 22x80d C6685
298. do. leaf-shaped C6691
299. do. 37x81x55 1997.28.9
300. do. 35x83x57 1997.28.8
301. do. 38x84x55
302. Game pie mould, tinplate & tinned copper embossed with gourgette and vegetables 111x242x139 A131
303. do. fluted sides 126x284x206 A132

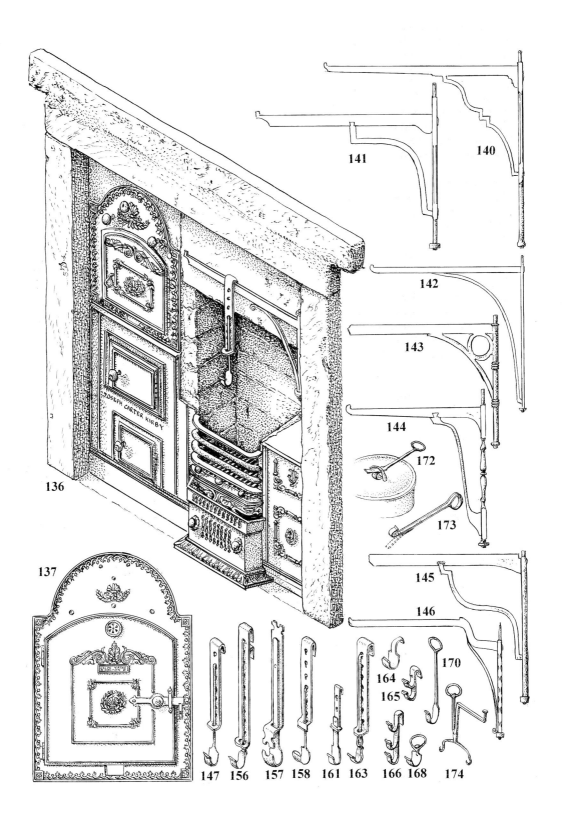

136

137

JOSEPH CARTER KIRBY

140

141

142

143

144

145

146

147 156 157 158 161 163 164 165 166 168 170 172 173 174

304 Waffle iron, cast iron plates riveted to wrought iron handles 818x164d x94 A189

305. Peel, wrought iron, blade riveted to handle 515x123d A927

306. do. 559x153d C9765

307. do. 695x130 C9767

308. do. wood blade bolted to ash shaft 1934x197x25d A138

309. do. wood 1528x240x21 C7281 Found by C.Farrow in a false roof at Douthwaite Hall

310. do. sheet iron blade welded to a sleeve, bolted onto an oval wooden shaft 1910x228x25 C7460

311. do. sheet iron riveted onto an iron sleeve, then riveted onto a round pine shaft 1662x211x33d A1601 Douthwaite Dale

312. do. sheet iron riveted to ash shaft   1825x210x33d C9076

Drink preparation

313. Water filter, buff glazed stoneware, the interior divided into three, the top for unfiltered water, the filter (beneath a fixed plate), and the bottom for filtered water. Applied plaques read;'BY HER MAJESTY'S ROYAL LETTERS PATENT (Royal arms)' and 'G.CHEAVINS/IMPROVED PATENT/GOLD MEDAL SELF CLEANING/RAPID WATER FILTER/BOSTON,ENGLAND', '42G', '6'. 450x253d A110

314. do. with additional plaque 'NEW PATENT/REMOVABLE/PLATE', 'G', 'R'. plate missing 458x256d C8394

315. do. with additional stamp 'D' 512x290at rim, with domed lid. C6220

316. do. buff glazed stoneware with 2 internal sections divided by a separate fixed plate. Exterior has 5 Greek-key rouletted bands, is stamped '0', and bears white applied plaques impressed in black 'ESTABLISHED 1830','COMPRESSED CHARCOAL/FILTER','SLACK & BROWNLOW', 'CANNING WORKS', 'MANCHESTER' 421x230d A109

317. Coffee mill, cast iron with spun brass hopper & turned rosewood knob on handle. Embossed octagonal brass plaque reads 'W.CROSS & SONS/WESTBROMWICH' 130h to rim x158x129 C5070

318. do. embossed oval brass plaque 'A.KENRICK & SONS/Royal arms/PATENT COFFEE MILL' 113h to rim x129x104 C5095

319. Coffee pot, tinplate, folded,seamed, with cast pewter knob and ebonised wooden handle 282x144d A94

320. Verjuice press, stone, 600x605

321. Brewing? jar, red earthenware, unglazed, with applied thumbed collar around the neck and pulled handles 264x208d C8808 This pot is virtually identical in form to one in the Yorkshire Museum See P.Brears *A Catalogue of English Country Pottery housed in the Yorkshire Museum* (York 1968) no. 95a, and forms part of a late medieval tradition continued in the 17th century by the Wedgwood family at Yearsley, and from the early to mid 19th centuries at the Heworth Moor pottery, York.

322. Spiggot, turned elm with box/ screw tap 285x67d C5953

323. do. turned sycamore with elm screw 238x82x39d C5954

324. do. turned elm with box? screw tap with cork lining 237x139x45d A6224

325. sycamore? tap only 123x73x27d C5955

326. Stoneware bottle, grey salt-glazed stoneware, impressed on plaque 'J&E WINDLE/PICKERING/322*3GALL' 433x224d C9620

327. do. but neck missing, and plaque terminates '488*2GALL' 350x207d C9712

328. do. brown stoneware, with white slip three-quarters down the body, a plaque stamped 'T.COVERDALE/KIRBYMOORSIDE/1 GALL' 315x164d. C9688

329. do. cylindrical body, iron-dipped conical shoulder 'T.COVERDALE/KIRBYMOORSIDE' 253x139 C9694

330. do. 'W.H.CALAM/KING'S HEAD HOTEL/KIRBYMOORSIDE' 307x162 C9117

331. do. 'F.STEPHENSON/WINE & SPIRIT MERCHANT/KIRBYMOORSIDE' 257x134 C9713

332. do. plus '1 GALL' 290x176d C5476

333. do. 'JAMES JACKSON/WINE & SPIRIT MERCHANT/KIRBYMOORSIDE' '892' 254x142d C9693

334. do. plus '805' and 'PEARSON/CHESTERFIELD' 315x176d C9692

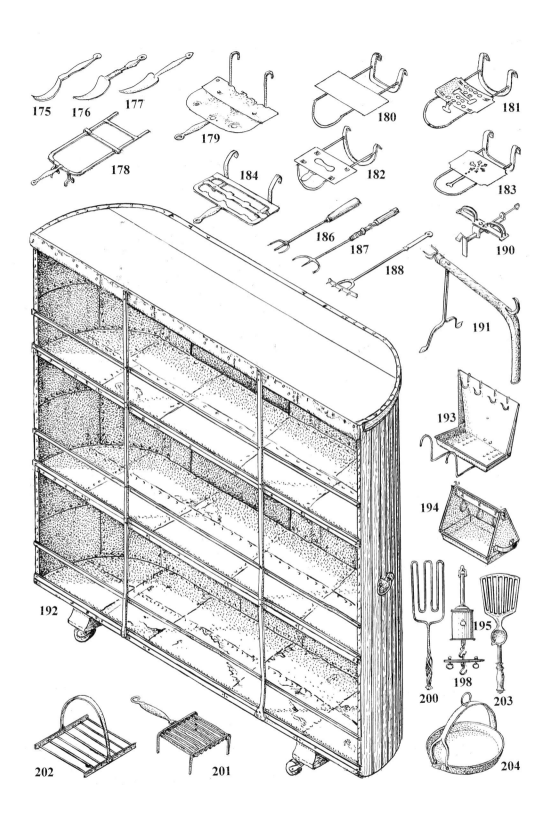

175 176 177

179

180

181

178

184

182

183

186 187

190

188

191

193

194

192

195

198

200

203

202 201

204

335. do. 'J.W.WALKER & CO/WINE & SPIRIT MERCHANTS/MALTON' 265x134d C5756
336. do. 'GEORGE PEACOCK/WINE & SPIRIT MERCHANT/ KIRBYMOORSIDE/2 GALL' '428' & impressed oval 'PEARSON & CO/WHITTINGTON MOOR/POTTERIES/NEAR CHESTERFIELD' 401x185d C9691
337. do. but impressed '672' and encased in a woven wicker casing 285x c170d
338. Codd bottle, pale green glass, moulded 'W.PEACOCK JUNr/VICTORIA ROAD/&/SEAMER ROAD/SCARBOROUGH' 217x65d 1992.32.5 Mrs Pettit, East Ayton, Scarborough
339. do. 'ATKINSON BROs/(picture of Helmsley Castle Keep)/ AERATED WATER MANFrs/ HELMSLEY', 'PATENT SAFE GROOVE/4/SOLE MAKERS/DAN RYLANDS Ld/BARNSLEY' 228x65d C7311
340. do. 'COVERDALE & SON/(rearing horse on barrel) TRADE MARK/ KIRBYMOORSIDE' 225x67 C7313
341-342. do. C7314 and C7314
343. do. 195x56d C7315
344. do. 'TRADE MARK/W.WALKER, KIRBYMOORSIDE YORKSHIRE/ REGISTERED' 'CODDS PATENT/RYLANDS & GOOD/MAKERS/BARNSLEY' 188x54d C7317
345. Glass bottle, cylindrical with domed base, moulded 'JOHN HARRISON/AERATED WATER/MANUFACTURER/KIRBYMOORSIDE' 238x58d C7327
346. do. 'STEVENSON/WHITBY' 237x60d C7328
347. do. champagne bottle shape 'ENGLISH/PICKERING 250x75d 1996.15.5 Mrs Preston, Thornton Dale
348. do. small convex-sided bottle 'JACKSON & SON/(horse on barrel)/TRADE MARK/Kirkby Moorside' 182x43d C7321
349-351. do. 217x61d C7332 & C7336
352. do, straight-sided with domed shoulder 'BLACK SWAN/PICKERING' 241x78d C7447
353. do. screwtop 'pop' bottle 'RUSSELLS & WRANGHAM LTD/BREWERS MALTON' 'DERWENT BREWERY TRADE MARK' and on the composition screw top 'RUSSELS & WRANGHAM/MALTON/LIMITED/R & W' 248x73d 1992.36.1 Mrs A Hutchinson, Hull, who picked it up on the moors at Blakey.

Liquid heating
354. Fountain, cast iron, the body moulded '...& Co, '4 GAL', cracked, and repaired with two bolted iron plates. Brass knob on lid & brass tap. 290x267d 80/24 T. Paul, Hovingham.
355. Kettle, copper, both body & spout seamed & raised, cast brass brackets and turned knob 285x100d A1005
356. do. 275x147d A1005
357. do. 234x168d A1006
358. do. cast brass bow handle, lid missing 315x180d A1000
359. do. sheet iron, wrought iron bow, later pressed tinplate lid 394x232d C5562
360. do. cast iron, lid missing, base moulded 'KENRICK & SONS 12 PINTS/ No 6' 33x218d A193
361. do. pressed tinplate lid, base moulded 'KENRICK & SONS/ 12 PINTS/PATENT/No6' 350x217d A192
362. do. pressed tinplate lid with brass knob, base moulded 'KENRICK & SONS/7 PINTS/No $3^1/_2$' 290x184d
363. do. base moulded 'KENRICK /4 PINTS' 230x142d C5708
364. do. domed cast iron lid, base moulded 'Hill Top Co/ 5 Quarts/ No 5' 317x198d C5563
365. Mull, copper, seamed & wire edged, tinned interior 297x134d C5174
366. do?. tinplate, 255x70d A942

Food serving
367. Breadboard, sycamore, turned rim carved with a garland and leaves 20x288d C6140
368. Butter dish stand, as no.364, with 'Butter' in gothic script included on border 17x159d C6140
369. do. 22x186d C6663
370-71. Salts, turned & varnished birch 66x66d at rim C6124 & C6125

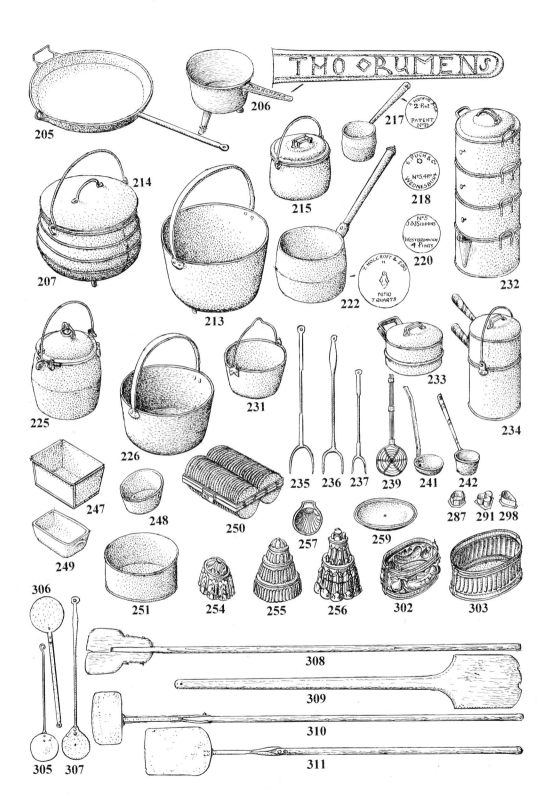

205

206

THO ◇ RUMENS

217

218

220

222

214

215

207

213

232

225

226

231

235 236 237 239 241 242

233

234

287 291 298

247

248

250

257

259

249

251 254 255 256 302 303

306

308

309

310

305 307 311

Food eating containers
372. Trencher, turned sycamore, 3 screw holes for chuck on back 20x198d C6143
373. do. ash? 4 screw holes 25x188d C6142
374. Pewter plate, single bead on rim, double stamped indistinctly...'HAMBERS' on the back, and 'R' and 'A S' on the rim C7649
375. do. stamped 'R' on rim 9x217d C7649
376-8 Soup plates, white glazed earthenware, blue transfer print on rim of running fox and 'ERYY' for the East Riding of Yorkshire Yeomanry. 38x258d 1997.29.7 a-c Mrs Maw, Kirkby Moorside
379. Egg cup, turned birch, 67x49d at rim C6117
380. do. oak, 83x62d at rim C6118
371. do. birch, varnished, 69x 51d at rim C119
382. do. wood 65x47d at rim C119
383. do. 73x45d at rim C6120
384. do. 58x47d at rim C6121
385. do. 69x50d at rim C6122
386. do. 60x47d at rim C6123

Cutlery
387-9 Table knives, steel, conical buffalo horn handle with domed end, tang riveted through a washer, blades stamped 'WARRANTED/JAMES RYALE/SHEFFIELD' 240x23d C5572 a-c
390. do. blade stamped 'VR/GEORGE...& COMPANY/TRINITY WORKS SHEFFIELD/ART' 236x24d C5572e
391. do. blade stamped 'DEPEND/W.SAYNOR & SONS/CUTLERS SHEFFIELD' 233x23d
392. do. blade stamped 'SLATER & PADGE/GRANTHAM' 238x23d C5572d
393. do. antler handle, blade stamped '...HAM & CO/...STREET/NEWCASTLE' 255x24 A2336
394. do. vegetable ivory? handle, tang riveted though brass washer 221x23 C5742
395. do. buffalo horn plates riveted on flat tang, blade stamped 'C+X/WARRANTED' 263x25 C8383
396. do. blade stamped 'WARDROBE & PEAS Co./SHEFFIELD' 241x24 C6390
397 do. cross-hatched bone scales riveted onto flat tang, blade stamped 'ART/WHITEHAVEN' 263x26 C8390
398. do. 259x26 C8387
399. do. blade stamped '(hunting horn)/HUNTER/SOLID CAST STEEL/SHEFFIELD' 254x22 C8389
400. do. blade stamped 'W & S BUTCHER/PHILADELPHIA P.../SHEFFIELD' 264x28 C8388
401-403. do. blades stamped ' V(crown)R/ GEORGE BUTLER & COMPANY/TRINITY WORKS SHEFFIELD' c.240x23 C8384 .
404. do. blade stamped'AARON BARROW & SONS/CUTLERS,SHEFFIELD' 265x24 C8386
405-6. do. blades stamped 'V(crown)R/ROBT. BAXTER & Co/SHEFFIELD 240x24 & 237x23 C8385
407. Table fork, two prongs, conical buffalo horn handle with domed end, tang riveted through a washer, 194x10 C6385
408, do. three prongs, haft stamped 'STEEL' 178x15 1991.2.9
409. do. 175x21d C5574
410. do. 172x23d C6327
411-412. do. 176x20d & 170x22d C8587
413-414. do. steel plates across butts 171x21 C5573a & 176x23 C5573b
415-418. do. buffalo horn handles with rectangular section, all c.174x14 A1665-7, C8142
419. do, 211x16 C6382
420. do. brass pin through handle 175x12 C6389
421. do. antler handle, riveted through washer, and brass pin through handle, 203x15 1990.27.9
422. do. end of tang riveted over 185x14 C8382
423. do. bone handle 207x15 A1668
424. do. four-pronged 171x13 C8140
425. do. 167x12 C5745

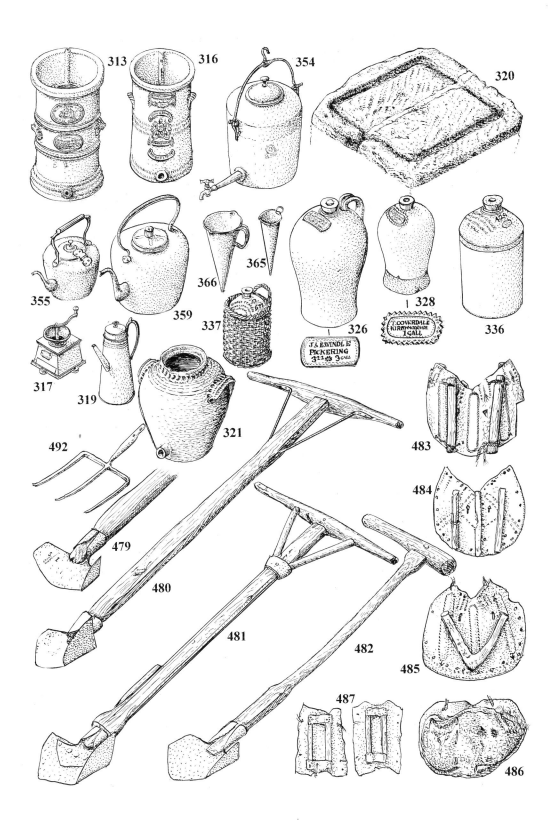

313 316 354 320
355 366 365 359 337 326 328 336
317 319 321 483
492 484
479 480 481 482 485
487 486
74

426. do. 171x11 C8140
427-432. do. cross-hatched bone scales riveted through flat tang, c. 198x13 C8380
433-434. do. c. 185x12 C6386
435. do. 180x13 C8381
436. do. three-pronged 177x13 A1566
437. Table fork carved from bone 159x15 C6391
438. Spoon, carved from bone 160x26 C6392
439. do. 117x21 C6393
440. do. 106x19 C6394
441. do. 123x16 C6395
442. do 119x22 C6396
443. do. 110x16 C6397
444. do. 99x17 C6398
445. do. 123x25 C6399
446. do. moulded creamware, stilt marks beneath bowl 205x45 A1008
447. Apple scoop, made from sheep shinbone 112x28 C6341
448. do. 100x25 C6370 used by T.Frank, Hutton le Hole
449. do. 121x28 C6369 from Spaunton
450. do 108x30 C6875
451. do. 115x28 C6373
452. do. decorated with a cross 107x 28 C6374
453. do. 109x27 C6371 used by T.Frank, Hutton le Hole
454. do. 106x25 C7307
455. do. 128x32 C6372

Drink service
456. Punch bowl, porcelain, incised '110' on the base, gilded bands and scrolls, an oval enamelled panel of a ship in full sail, and remains of the inscription; 'Presented to Miss Elizabeth Andrews/ Success to the "Mary Eliza" of Whitby/ Captain: Joseph Harrison, 1854' 137x147 1991.13.1 The 'Mary Eliza' was a Whitby whaler, her Captain married Miss Andrews and their son John Andrew ('Jodo') Harrison had a mineral-water business in Kirkby Moorside. The bowl was presented by Mrs Bottomley, his grand-daughter. Known as Elsinor bowls, they were made in Denmark for visiting vessels during their periods of re-loading.
457. Punch ladle, wood, turned bowl on integral carved stem, which incorporates a hook to fit the rim of the bowl. 318x62d C6147
458. Teapot, cast Britannia metal, soldered, engraved, ivory knob & ceramic insulation rings. Stamped 'H.C.& Co. S/1990' on base 155x252x109 A107
459. do. cast, spun, stamped and soldered, black ceramic insulation rings 181x248x145 A106

Drinking vessels
460. Horn mug 119x55d A1876
461. do. 115x55 A1877
462 do. 113x55 A1878 from Appleton le Moor
463. do. 116x53 A1879
464. do 102x47 A1880 from Kirkby Moorside
465. do. 99x50 A1881 from Helmsley
466. Mug, pearlware, two handles, green transfer print including 'LOVE FEAST' with floral sprigs on one side, and a romantic scene of a rustic bridge, castle etc. on the other. 117x123d C8799 from the Primitive Methodist Chapel, Wombleton
467. Mug, white glazed earthenware with one handle, cobalt blue sponge decoration 127x136d C8798 Loving cup from Danby
468. do. blue border and green cross sponge decoration 89x93d A1101
469. do. blue crescents and sprays of three flower sponging on upper & lower borders, central sponged band of pink flowers and leaves 97x88d

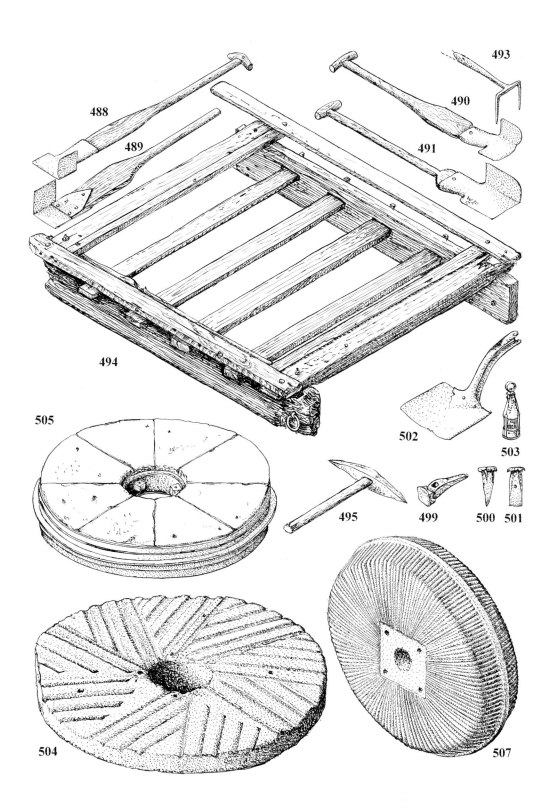

488

489

490

491

493

494

505

502

503

495

499

500 501

504

507

470-72. do. pale blue banding and transfer printed cartouch 'WESLEYAN SUNDAY/SCHOOL/ GILLAMOOR' c.90x91d A1102-4

473-4. Tea cups, bone china, with black transfer prints 'ROSEDALE ABBEY. NORTH VIEW' and gilt band down handle c.75x45d C8800 & C11380

475-6. Saucers matching the above, transferred 'WAGSTAFF & BRUNT/LONGTON' 25x147d C8800b & C11380 This company operated from 1880 to 1927, making many souvenir and commemorative wares

477. Tea-plate, matching the above, 15x158d C8800c

478. Tea cup, Devon red-bodied polychrome slipware, with sgraffito cottage & 'HUTTON-LE-HOLE' & 'Heaven send thee/many merry days' 73x51d 1992.44.1

Fuel

479. Peat Cock spade, ash? handle cut from a natural fork, iron blade stamped 'C.T.SKE.../SHEFFIELD' 'S'   1715x667x140height of vertical blade. Used by Tom Frank of Hutton le Hole up to the 1920s

480. do. pine, 1730x698x134h C7441

481. do. 1702x723x168h C7442

482. do. Thigh spade, ash? shaft with pine crosspiece 1460x390x75h C7443

483. Knapper, leather with pierced decoration and wooden battens tied to the front 390x400xc.30

484. do. with battens nailed on 408x380xc.30 C30

485. do. with wooden fork on the front, and sacking padded with wool on the back 348x440xc.50 A22 from Low Wold House, Farndale

486. do. 450x440 A21 from Hutton le Hole

487. do. leather, made from a pair of old leggings, each mounted with a wooden frame 315x240xc.20 A19/1 & 300x230xc.20 A19/2 used by Tom Frank of Hutton le Hole

488. Peat spade, wrought iron on ash? shaft 1015x160x95 A23 used at the Lion Inn at Blakey

489. do. 935x109x98 C9084

490. do. ash crosspiece on elm shaft 885x130x101 C7282

491. do. ash? shaft 922x160x105 C7289 used by a Hutton le Hole man on the peat bog on Rosedale Moor

492. Turf fork, wrought iron 229x132 A30 from Farndale

493. Turf rake, wrought iron 180x13x19 A29 from Farndale

494. Turf sledge, 315x1586x1225

495. Coal pick, wrought iron with ash handle 470l. head 61x44x396 C7435

496. do. head only, 58x47x402 C7401 from Blakey

497. do. 6-pointed star in circle stamped on top 64x39x430 C7400 from Blakey

498. do. 56x40x374 C7399

499. Hammer head, wrought iron 60x65x223 C7405

500. Wedge, wrought iron, pointed 160x62x40 C7403 from Blakey

501. do, with straight blade 153x50x47 C7388 from Blakey

502. Shovel, wrought iron, 520x269 C7388 from Blakey

503. Lamp, tinplate, soldered, with pierced ventilation holes & cylindrical glass 220x67d C7385 from Rudland Rigg coal mines

Milling

504. Millstone, 160x1080d

505-6. do. composite French burr stones mounted in iron bands. Bedstone 125x860d Runner 125x905d

507. Pearling mill stone 195x860d C11520

Notes

Introduction
1. T.Hearne, *Itinerary of John Leland the Antiquary* (1745) I 64-5
2. Handbill dated 2-10 August, 1935, RFM

Traditional Cookery
1. B.Frank 'Salt Boxes of the North York Moors' *Dalesman* (Clapham, North Yorks.1970) December issue
2. P.Brears, *Catalogue of English Country Pottery housed in the Yorkshire Museum, York* (York 1968) pp 19 & 31
3. W.Marshall, *The Rural Economy of Yorkshire* (1788) II 347
4. Mrs Gutch, *The Folk-lore of Yorkshire, North Riding...* (1901) 220
5. A.Hunter, *Culina Famulatrix Medicinae* 4th ed. (York 1806) 110
6. W.Marshall, 316
7. J.Tuke, *General View of the Agriculture of the North Riding of Yorkshire* (1800) 117
8. Castle Museum, York. Letter to Dr Kirk from John S.Gaynor, then of New Earswick, 6th Nov.,1928
9. J.Tuke, 117
10. J.Tuke, 116
11. Woodcock, H. *Primitive Methodism on the Yorkshire Wolds* (1889) 22
12. W.Marshall, 359 & 361
13. Harriet Fox *1735 Recipe Book*, Leeds Archives Dept. LF134 quoted in P.Brears, *The Gentlewoman's Kitchen* (Wakefield 1984) 61
14. R.Blakeborough, *Yorkshire Wit, Character, Folklore and Custom* (1898) 347
15. M.Heavisides, *Rambles in Cleveland* (1901) 42
16. M.Heavisides, 67

Farmhouse Food
1. W.J.Halliday & A.S.Umpleby, *The White Rose Garland* (1949) 116
2. for further information on the food in East Riding farms see P.Brears, *Traditional Food in Yorkshire* (Edinburgh 1987) 27-34
3. W.Marshall, *The Rural Economy of Yorkshire* (1788) 259
4. B.Frank, *Life in Ryedale* (Hutton le Hole 1986) 35
5. ibid.34-35
6. J.C.Atkinson, *Glossary of the Cleveland Dialect* (1868) 36
7. P.Hutchinson, *Old English Cookery* (1993) 39
8. P.Hutchinson, *Peggy Hutchinson's Preserving Secrets* (n.d.) 64

Traditional Celebrations
1. P.Brears, *Traditional Food in Yorkshire* (Edinburgh 1987) 163
2. ibid. 162
3. ibid. 164
4. M.Newbery, *Reminiscences of a Bradford Mill Girl* (Bradford 1980) 7
5. A, Brooke, *Slingsby & Slingsby Castle* (1904) 240
6. H.J.& B.M.Walker, *Recollections* (Leeds 1934) 17
7. M.Chapman & P.Smith, *North Yorkshire Within Living Memory* (Newbury 1995) 80
8. W.Marshall, *The Rural Economy of Yorkshire* (1788) II 'Mell Supper' in his glossary
9. M.C.F.Morris, *Yorkshire Folk Talk* (1892) 214
10. Mrs Gutch, *County Folk-lore, East Riding of Yorkshire* (London 1911) 104-5
11. Anon. *The Trial & Life of Eugene Aram* (Richmond, Yorks., 1832) 113
12. J.C.Atkinson, *A Glossary of the Cleveland Dialect* (1868) 292
13. M.Hartley & J.Ingilby, *Life in the Moorlands of North-East Yorkshire* (1972) 59
14. F.Tweddell, *Rhymes & Sketches to Illustrate the Cleveland Dialect* (Stokesley 1892) 11-12
15. RFM no. C9789
16. RFM no. C9189
17. RFM no. 10689

18. J.C.Atkinson, 377
19.RFM no. 1997.7.1
20. Mrs Gutch, 273, & *The Gentleman's Magazine* (1824) part II 588
21. Fir further details see P. Brears, *Traditional Food in Yorkshire* (Edinburgh 1987)183-196
22. R.Blakeborough, *Yorkshire Wit, Character, Folklore & Custom* (1898) 117 & J.C.Atkinson, *40 Years in a Moorland Parish* (1891) 227-9

'Lowance Time' on threshing day at Oxclose Farm, Hutton le Hole, taken by William Hayes in 1948.

George Collier cutting turf on Blakey Moor in 1936 using a cock spade, and protecting his thighs with a 'knapper' of wood and leather. The stacks of drying turves can be seen on the moorland behind him.

Index of Recipes